GCSE

Biology

There are only three ways to make sure you're fully prepared for the
Grade 9-1 GCSE Biology exams — practice, practice and ~~knitting~~ practice.

That's why we've packed this brilliant CGP book with realistic exam-style
questions on every topic. All the required practicals are covered too and
there are plenty of targeted analysis questions to test those tricky AO3 skills.

You'll also find step-by-step answers at the back, to easily check your work
and find out how to pick up any marks you missed out on. Splendid!

Exam Practice Workbook
Higher Level

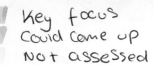

Key focus
Could come up
Not assessed

Contents

☑ Use the tick boxes to check off the topics you've completed.

Topic 7 — Ecology

Mixed Questions

Answers

You can find some useful information about What to Expect in the Exams and other exam tips at cgpbooks.co.uk/GCSEBiologyHigher/Exams

Published by CGP

Editors:
Luke Bennett, Eleanor Crabtree, Mary Falkner, Chris Lindle, Sarah Pattison, Rachael Rogers, Camilla Sheridan.

Contributors:
Sophie Anderson, Helen Brace, James Foster, Bethan Parry, Alison Popperwell.

With thanks to Susan Alexander and Glenn Rogers for the proofreading.

With thanks to Lottie Edwards for the copyright research.

Data in Figure 1 on page 34 source: Health Survey for England 2018. Licensed under the Open Government Licence v3.0
http://www.nationalarchives.gov.uk/doc/open-government-licence/version/3/

Data in Figure 2 on page 34 contains information from NHS Digital. Licensed under the Open Government Licence v3.0
http://www.nationalarchives.gov.uk/doc/open-government-licence/version/3/

Clipart from Corel®
Illustrations by: Sandy Gardner Artist, email sandy@sandygardner.co.uk
Printed by Elanders Ltd, Newcastle upon Tyne

Based on the classic CGP style created by Richard Parsons.

How to Use This Book

- Hold the book <u>upright</u>, approximately <u>50 cm</u> from your face, ensuring that the text looks like <u>this</u>, not ˢᴉɥʇ. Alternatively, place the book on a <u>horizontal</u> surface (e.g. a table or desk) and sit adjacent to the book, at a distance which doesn't make the text too small to read.

- Before attempting to use this book, familiarise yourself with the following <u>safety information</u>:

There are warm-up questions for the trickier sub-topics, to ease you in and get you thinking along the right lines.

These grade stamps help to show how difficult the questions are. Remember, to get a top grade you need to be able to answer <u>all</u> the questions, not just the hardest ones.

20% of marks in the real exams test analytical skills that come under Assessment Objective 3 (AO3). AO3 skills include evaluating data, drawing conclusions and suggesting ways to improve procedures. The skills needed to earn these precious AO3 marks are easily overlooked, so sections targeting these skills are marked up like this.

You'll have done some 'required practical activities' as part of your course, and you could be asked about any of them in your exams. Whenever one of the required practical activities crops up in this book, it's marked up like this.

In the real exams, some questions will be marked using a 'levels of response' mark scheme. In this book, these questions are marked with an asterisk (*). You'll be marked on the <u>overall quality</u> of your answer, so make sure you give a full, detailed answer that is logical and coherent.

You're told how many marks each question part is worth, and then the total for the whole question.

Exam Tips give you hints to help with answering exam questions.

Tick the box that matches how confident you feel with the questions in each sub-topic. This should help show you where you need to focus your revision.

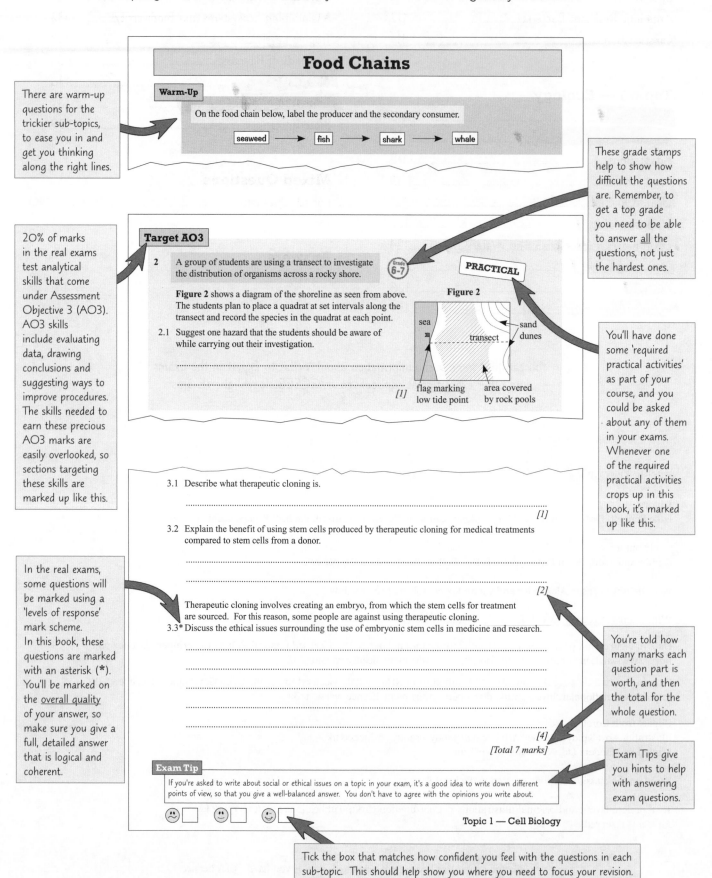

Food Chains

Warm-Up

On the food chain below, label the producer and the secondary consumer.

seaweed → fish → shark → whale

Target AO3

2   A group of students are using a transect to investigate the distribution of organisms across a rocky shore. *(Grade 6-7)*   PRACTICAL

Figure 2 shows a diagram of the shoreline as seen from above. The students plan to place a quadrat at set intervals along the transect and record the species in the quadrat at each point.

2.1   Suggest one hazard that the students should be aware of while carrying out their investigation.

....

....   *[1]*

Figure 2

sea — sand dunes — transect — flag marking low tide point — area covered by rock pools

3.1   Describe what therapeutic cloning is.

....   *[1]*

3.2   Explain the benefit of using stem cells produced by therapeutic cloning for medical treatments compared to stem cells from a donor.

....

....   *[2]*

Therapeutic cloning involves creating an embryo, from which the stem cells for treatment are sourced. For this reason, some people are against using therapeutic cloning.

3.3*   Discuss the ethical issues surrounding the use of embryonic stem cells in medicine and research.

....

....

....

....

....   *[4]*

[Total 7 marks]

Exam Tip

If you're asked to write about social or ethical issues on a topic in your exam, it's a good idea to write down different points of view, so that you give a well-balanced answer. You don't have to agree with the opinions you write about.

☹ ☐   ☺ ☐   ☺ ☐

Topic 1 — Cell Biology

Cells

Use the words on the right to correctly fill in the gaps in the passage.
You don't have to use every word, but each word can only be used once.

many
smaller
plant
bacterial
single   larger
animal
simpler

Most eukaryotic organisms are made up of ......many...... cells.
They include ......Plant...... and ......animal...... cells.
Prokaryotic organisms are ...Single bacteria...... cells. They are
......Bacteria simpler...... and ......smaller...... than eukaryotic cells.

1   **Figure 1** shows a diagram of an animal cell.   Grade 4-6

Figure 1

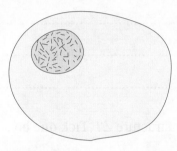

1.1   Label the cell membrane, cytoplasm and nucleus on **Figure 1**.

[3]

1.2   Give the function of each part of the cell on **Figure 1**.

Cell membrane ......Controls what enters and exits the cell......

Cytoplasm ......where most chemical reaction occour......

Nucleus ......Controls the cell activity of the cell......

[3]

1.3   Name **two** other subcellular structures that can be found in an animal cell.
Describe the function of each structure.

......mitochondria - aerobic respiration......

......ribosome - protein synthesis......

......

[4]

1.4   Give **one** reason why the diagram in **Figure 1** does not represent a plant cell.

......dosen't have a cell wall......

[1]

[Total 11 marks]

2 **Figure 2** shows a diagram of a prokaryotic cell.

Figure 2

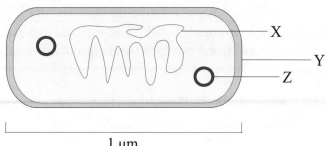

1 μm

2.1 Which of the following is a prokaryotic cell?
Tick **one** box.

☐ root hair cell   ☑ bacterium   ☐ sperm   ☐ nerve cell

[1]

2.2 Name structures X, Y and Z on **Figure 2**.

X .....DNA.....

Y .....Cell wall.....

Z .....Plasmid.....

[3]

2.3 Which of the following is true for structure Z? Tick **one** box.

☐ It is where photosynthesis occurs.

☐ It is part of the cell membrane.

☑ It contains genetic material.

[1]

Look at the scale on **Figure 2**.
2.4 A eukaryotic cell measures 10 μm long.
How many times larger is it than the cell in **Figure 2**?

.....10.....

[1]

2.5 The head of a pin is approximately 1 mm in diameter.
How many prokaryotic cells would fit lengthways across it?

1×10^{-3} $\begin{matrix} 1\mu m \\ 1 \times 10^{-6} \end{matrix}$ $-3--6 = -3+6 = 3$

1×10^3 1000

.....1000..... cells

[2]

2.6 Give **one** difference between prokaryotic and eukaryotic cells, other than their size.

.....eukaryotic cells have DNA enclosed in a nucleus.....
.....whereas prokaryotic cells don't have DNA enclosed in.....
.....a nucleus.....

[1]

[Total 9 marks]

Microscopy

1 A student observed blood cells under a microscope.
A scale drawing of one of the cells is shown in **Figure 1**.

Figure 1

A

In **Figure 1**, A is the image width. The real width of the cell is 0.012 mm.
What is the magnification of the image? Use the formula:

$$\text{magnification} = \frac{\text{size of image}}{\text{size of real object}}$$

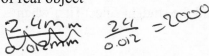

$$\frac{2.4mm}{0.012mm} \qquad \frac{24}{0.012} = 2000$$

magnification = × 2000

[Total 2 marks]

2 A plant cell is magnified 1000 times using a light microscope.

2.1 The length of the image of the plant cell is 10 mm.
Calculate the actual length of one plant cell in millimetres (mm). Use the formula:

$$\text{magnification} = \frac{\text{size of image}}{\text{size of real object}}$$

$$1000 = \frac{10mm}{real} \qquad \frac{10}{1000} =$$

0.01 mm

[2]

2.2 What is the length of one plant cell in micrometres (μm)?

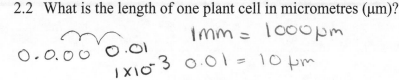

0.0.00 0.01
1×10⁻³   0.01 = 10 μm

1mm = 1000μm

0.00001 10 μm

[1]

2.3 How do magnification and resolution compare between electron and light microscopes?

electron microscopes have a ~~large~~ higher magnification
and resolution than light microscopes

[2]

2.4 Explain how electron microscopy has increased understanding of subcellular structures.

allow Scientists to see small structures inside
a cell e.g. ribosome and can be seen with a
greater detail

[2]

[Total 7 marks]

Topic 1 — Cell Biology

More on Microscopy

1   A student wants to use a light microscope to view a sample of onion cells.   **Grade 4-6**

1.1   The student adds a drop of iodine stain to her sample. Which statement best describes when a stain might be used to view a sample of tissue? Tick **one** box.

☐   When the specimen is too thick for light to pass through.

☑   When the specimen is colourless.

☐   When there aren't many sub-cellular structures present in the cells.

☐   When a cover slip is not being used.

[1]

Figure 1 shows a diagram of the light microscope that the student plans to use.

1.2   The three different objective lenses are labelled in **Figure 1** with their magnification. Which lens should the student select first when viewing her cells?

.... × 4 ....

[1]

Figure 1

× 10

× 40

× 4

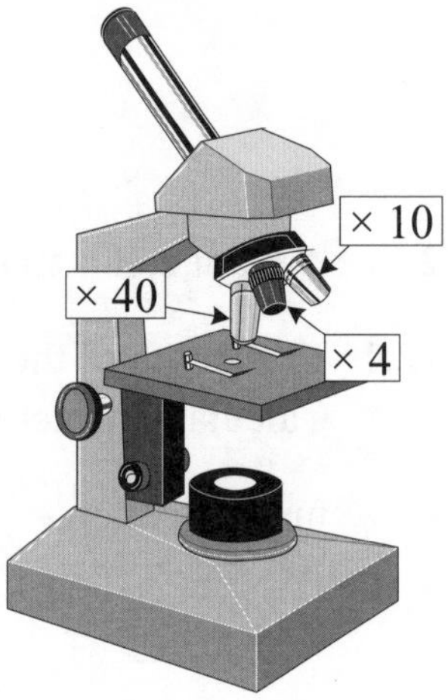

1.3   After she has selected the objective lens, she looks down the eyepiece and uses the adjustment knobs. Describe the purpose of the adjustment knobs.

....

....

....

[1]

1.4   The student wants to see the cells at a greater magnification. Describe the steps that she should take.

....

....

....

[2]

1.5   After she has viewed the cells, she wants to produce a scientific drawing of them. Her teacher has advised her to use clear, unbroken lines to draw the structures she can see. Give **two** other ways in which she can ensure she produces an accurate and useful drawing.

1. ...Colour in the Structures...

2. ....

[2]

[Total 7 marks]

Exam Tip

Make sure you pay attention to the number of marks that a question is worth. For some questions, they're a bit like a secret tip from the examiners about how much they want you to write. For example, if a 'describe' question is worth two marks, you'll usually need to make two separate points to get full marks. So check you're happy with your answers.

Topic 1 — Cell Biology

 ☐   ☐   ☐

Cell Differentiation and Specialisation

Different types of cell have different structures that help them carry out specific functions. Draw arrows below to match up each type of plant cell with its structure and function.

Plant cell

Structure and Function

root hair cell

xylem

phloem

Very few subcellular structures and holes in the end cell walls allow dissolved sugars to move from one cell to the next.

Lots of chloroplasts for absorption of sunlight.

Cells that are hollow in the centre and have no end cell walls form a continuous tube for transporting water from roots to leaves.

Long finger-like projection increases surface area for absorption of water.

1 As an organism develops, some of its cells develop different structures and change into different types of cells. This allows the cells to carry out specific functions. What is this process called? Tick **one** box.

Grade 4-6

☐ mitosis　　☐ adaptation　　☑ differentiation　　☐ specialisation

[Total 1 mark]

2 Sperm cells are specialised to help them achieve their function. **Figure 1** shows the structure of a sperm cell.

Grade 6-7

Figure 1

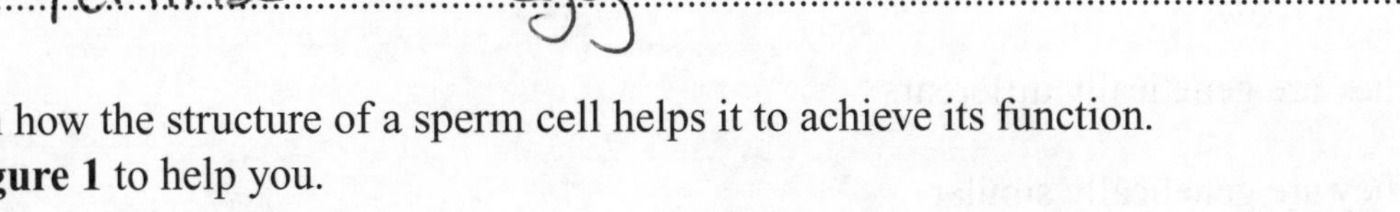

lots of mitochondria

long tail

streamlined head

head contains enzymes

2.1 What is the function of a sperm cell?

to fertilise an egg

[1]

2.2 Explain how the structure of a sperm cell helps it to achieve its function. Use **Figure 1** to help you.

lots of mitochondria provides energy for movement.
tail aids the sperm swim.
Enzyme in the head allows it to bre digest
the egg.

[4]

[Total 5 marks]

Topic 1 — Cell Biology

Chromosomes and Mitosis

1   **Figure 1** shows different stages of the cell cycle.

Figure 1

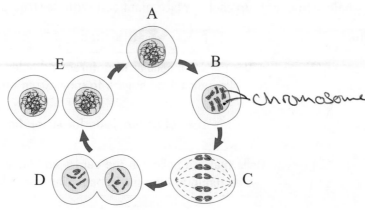

→ Chromosome

1.1   Label the chromosomes on cell B.

[1]

1.2   Name the chemical molecule that chromosomes are made of.

DNA

[1]

1.3   Cell A is preparing to divide. What is happening to the cell?
Tick **two** boxes.

☐ The nucleus is dividing.   ☑ The number of subcellular structures is increasing.   ☐ The chromosomes are splitting.

☐ The cytoplasm is dividing.   ☑ The chromosomes are doubling.

[2]

1.4   Describe what is happening to cell D.

Cell membrane and cytoplasm are splitting apart

[2]

1.5   How do the two cells produced at stage E compare to parent cell A?
Tick **one** box.

☐ They are genetically different.

☐ They are genetically similar.

☑ They are genetically identical.

[1]

[Total 7 marks]

Exam Tip

In the exam, you might be asked to interpret what's going on in photos of real cells undergoing mitosis. Don't panic if the cells themselves don't look familiar — the main thing you have to look at is what the chromosomes are doing.

Topic 1 — Cell Biology

Binary Fission

1 Scientists performed an experiment to observe the growth of bacteria in a nutrient broth at 25 °C. **Table 1** shows their results.

Table 1

Time (hours)	0	2	4	6	8	10	12	14	16
Absorbance (au)	0.01	0.05	0.10	0.20	0.40	0.66	0.78	0.80	0.80

1.1 Use the data in **Table 1** to finish plotting **Figure 1** and draw a line of best fit.

Figure 1

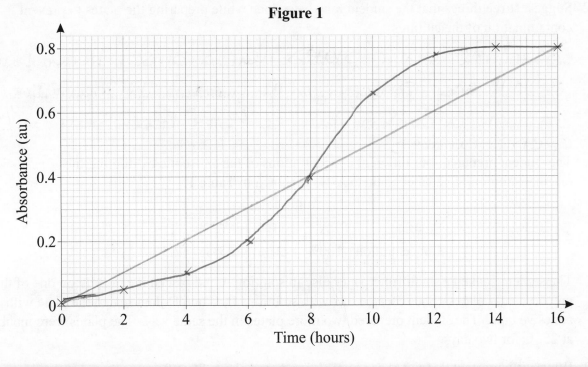

[3]

1.2 The absorbance increases because the bacteria are dividing. What type of cell division is occurring?

.....binary.......fission...

[1]

1.3 Suggest **one** factor that might be limiting the population growth after 14 hours.

...~~nutience~~...amount..of..nutrience...

[1]

[Total 5 marks]

2 A type of bacteria was found to have a mean division time of <u>45 minutes</u> at 20 °C. If one of these bacteria was given the same conditions, how many bacteria would there be in the population after <u>9 hours</u>? Give your answer in standard form.

9 hrs = $\frac{540 \text{ mins}}{45}$ = 12

$2^{12} = 4096$

4.096×10^3

Number of bacteria = ...

[Total 4 marks]

Topic 1 — Cell Biology

Culturing Microorganisms

1 A student was investigating the effect of different concentrations of an antiseptic on the growth of *Bacillus subtilis* bacteria.

Grade 6-7

1.1 The student prepared uncontaminated cultures of the bacteria on agar plates.
Why was it important that the cultures were not contaminated?

Could affect the growth of bacteria and Contamination could have cause the growth of a Pathogen

[2]

1.2 Suggest **three** things that the student may have done while preparing the plates to prevent contamination of the cultures.

open the agar plates near a bunsen burner flame to kill any Pathogen in the air. run the inoculating loop through a bunsen burner flame. used sterilised petri dishes

[3]

The student prepared four different concentrations of the antiseptic by diluting the original solution. She labelled them A-D, as shown in **Table 1**.

Table 1

Solution	A	B	C	D
Concentration	100%	50%	25%	12.5%

The student soaked a small filter paper disc in solution A and placed it carefully on one of the prepared agar plates. She repeated this with solutions B, C and D then sealed the plate with adhesive tape. The student prepared two more plates in the same way. The plates were incubated at 25 °C for two days.

1.3 Why is it important that the plates weren't incubated above 25 °C?

reduces the chance of a harmful Pathor~bacteria~ growing.

[1]

After two days, the student measured the diameters of the inhibition zones around the discs. The results are shown in **Table 2**.

Table 2

	Solution	A	B	C	D
Diameter (mm)	Plate 1	17	10	7	7
	Plate 2	19	15	8	5
	Plate 3	15	14	12	6
	Mean	17	X	9	6

1.4 Calculate the value of **X** in **Table 2**.

X = *13* mm

[1]

The student repeated the experiment using a different antiseptic.
The results are summarised in **Table 3**.

Table 3

Concentration of solution	100%	50%	25%	12.5%
Mean radius (mm)	11	8	5	4
Area of inhibition zone (cm²)	3.8	2.0	Y	0.5

1.5 Calculate the value of Y to complete **Table 3**.
Use the formula πr^2, where $\pi = 3.14$. Give your answer in cm^2.

$$5mm = 0.5cm$$
$$\pi \times 0.5^2$$

Y = ~~78.5~~ ~~0.8~~ 7.9 cm²

[2]

1.6 Use **Table 3** to plot a graph of the area of the inhibition zone against the concentration of the
solution for the 100%, 50% and 12.5% solutions. Draw a line of best fit between the points.

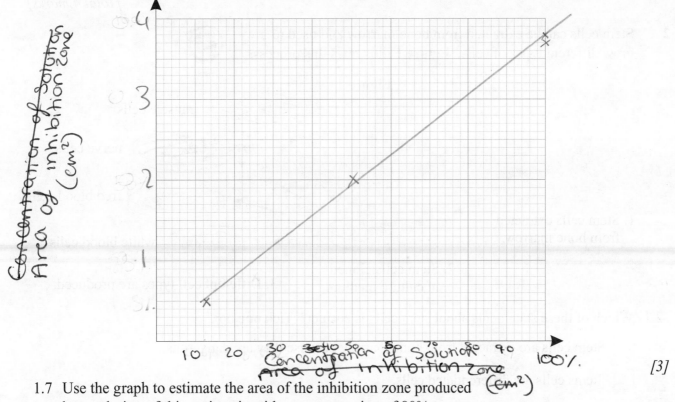

[3]

1.7 Use the graph to estimate the area of the inhibition zone produced
by a solution of this antiseptic with a concentration of 80%.

3.1

[1]

1.8 Describe the relationship between the concentration of antiseptic and its effectiveness
at preventing bacterial growth.

as concentration increases, the effectiveness increases.

[1]

[Total 14 marks]

Exam Tip

If you need to draw a graph in the exam, make sure you pick a scale that means your graph covers at least half of the
graph paper — if your scale is too small it'll be difficult to plot the points correctly and you might miss out on marks.

Topic 1 — Cell Biology

Stem Cells

1   Stem cells can be found in the growing areas of plants.   Grade 4-6

1.1   What are these growing areas of a plant called?
Tick **one** box.

☐ cloning zones   ☐ meristems   ☐ leaves   ☐ mesophyll layers

[1]

1.2   You can produce cloned plants from plant stem cells.
Describe **three** benefits of producing cloned plants from stem cells.

....

....

....

[3]

[Total 4 marks]

2   Stem cells can be extracted from bone marrow and used to grow different types of cells. **Figure 1** illustrates this process.   Grade 6-7

Figure 1

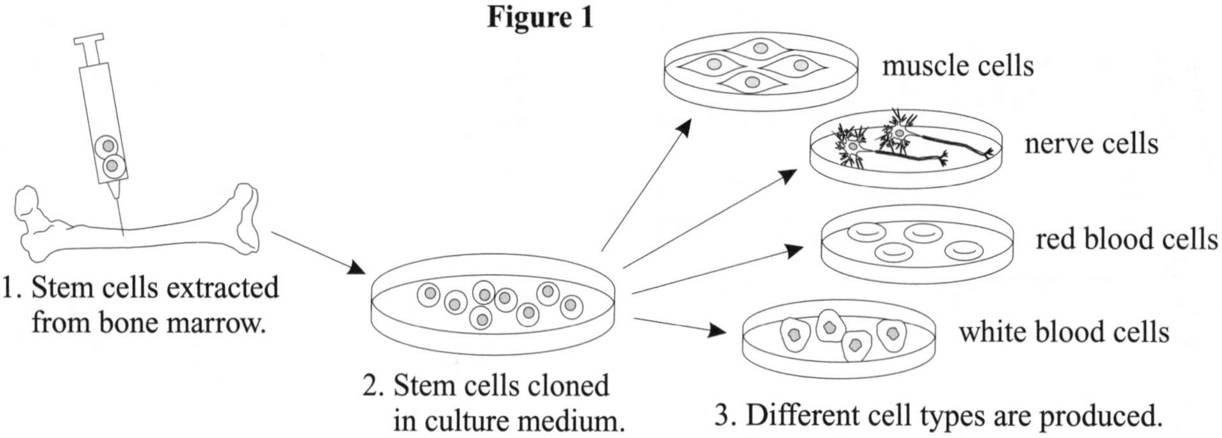

1. Stem cells extracted from bone marrow.

2. Stem cells cloned in culture medium.

3. Different cell types are produced.

muscle cells

nerve cells

red blood cells

white blood cells

2.1   Which of these statements about stem cells is correct? Tick **one** box.

☐ Stem cells are extracted from bone marrow because they are dangerous.

☐ Stems cells are differentiated cells.

☐ Stem cells can be found in every organ of the body.

☐ Stem cells can differentiate into many types of body cell.

[1]

2.2   Why are the stem cells cloned?

....

[1]

2.3   Why can't all body cells be used to grow different types of cell?

....

....

[1]

Topic 1 — Cell Biology

The technique shown in **Figure 1** could be used to produce cells for some medical treatments.

2.4 Besides bone marrow, where else can stem cells for medical treatments be obtained from?

....

[1]

2.5 Name **one** medical condition that may be helped by treatment using stem cells.

....

[1]

2.6 Give **one** potential risk of using stem cells in medical treatments.

....

[1]

[Total 6 marks]

3   **Figure 2** shows the process of therapeutic cloning.   (Grade 7-9)

Figure 2

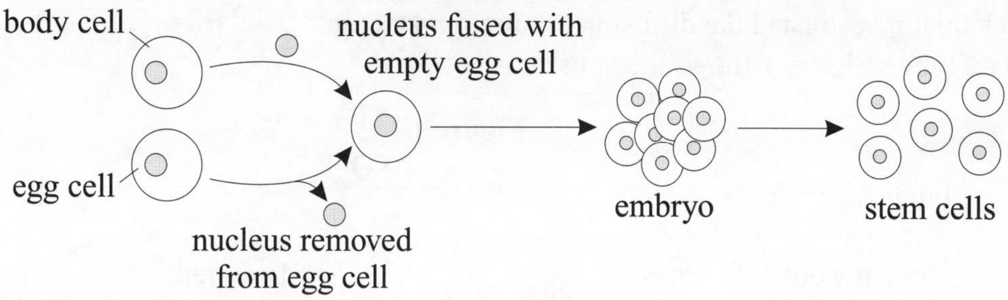

3.1 Describe what therapeutic cloning is.

....

[1]

3.2 Explain the benefit of using stem cells produced by therapeutic cloning for medical treatments compared to stem cells from a donor.

....

....

[2]

Therapeutic cloning involves creating an embryo, from which the stem cells for treatment are sourced. For this reason, some people are against using therapeutic cloning.

3.3* Discuss the ethical issues surrounding the use of embryonic stem cells in medicine and research.

....

....

....

....

....

[4]

[Total 7 marks]

Exam Tip

If you're asked to write about social or ethical issues on a topic in your exam, it's a good idea to write down different points of view, so that you give a well-balanced answer. You don't have to agree with the opinions you write about.

Diffusion

Warm-Up

The diagram on the right shows three cells. The carbon dioxide concentration inside each cell is shown. Draw arrows between the cells to show in which directions the carbon dioxide will diffuse.

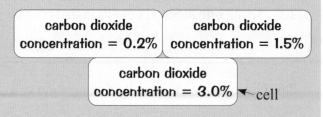

carbon dioxide concentration = 0.2%   carbon dioxide concentration = 1.5%

carbon dioxide concentration = 3.0% ◄ cell

1 Which of these molecules is not able to diffuse through a cell membrane? Tick **one** box.

☐ protein   ☐ oxygen   ☐ glucose   ☐ water

[Total 1 mark]

2 A scientist investigated the diffusion of ammonia along a glass tube. **Figure 1** shows the apparatus she used.

Figure 1

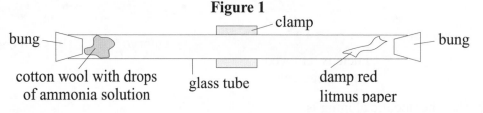

bung — clamp

cotton wool with drops of ammonia solution   glass tube   damp red litmus paper   bung

When the ammonia reaches the end of the tube, the litmus paper changes colour. The scientist timed how long this colour change took at five different concentrations of ammonia. **Table 1** shows her results.

Table 1

Concentration of ammonia (number of drops)	1	2	3	4	5
Time (s)	46	35	28	19	12

2.1 Define diffusion in terms of the particles of a gas.

....

....

[3]

2.2 What do the results in **Table 1** show about the effect of concentration on the rate of diffusion?

....

[1]

2.3 State **two** factors, other than concentration gradient, that affect the rate of diffusion into a cell.

....

....

[2]

2.4 Suggest how the scientist could increase the precision of her results.

....

[1]

[Total 7 marks]

Topic 1 — Cell Biology

Osmosis

1 Osmosis is a form of diffusion. (Grade 4-6)

1.1 Define osmosis.

....

....

....

[3]

1.2 In which of these is osmosis occurring? Tick **one** box.

☐ A plant is absorbing water from the soil.

☐ Sugar is being taken up into the blood from the gut.

☐ Water is evaporating from a leaf.

☐ Oxygen is entering the blood from the lungs.

[1]

[Total 4 marks]

PRACTICAL

2 A student did an experiment to see the effect of different salt solutions on pieces of potato. He cut five equal-sized rectangular chips from a raw potato and determined the mass of each chip. Each chip was placed in a beaker containing a different concentration of salt solution. The mass of each chip was measured again after 24 hours. The results are shown in **Table 1**. (Grade 6-7)

Table 1

Beaker	1	2	3	4	5
Concentration of salt solution (%)	0	1	2	5	10
Mass of potato chip at start of experiment (g)	5.70	5.73	5.71	5.75	5.77
Mass of potato chip after 24 hours (g)	6.71	6.58	6.27	5.46	4.63

2.1 Explain why it is important that all the potato pieces come from the same potato.

....

[1]

2.2 Calculate the percentage change in mass after 24 hours for the potato chip in beaker 2.

.... %

[2]

2.3 The student wanted to find a solution that would not cause the mass of the chip to change. Suggest what concentration of salt solution the student should try.

....

[1]

[Total 4 marks]

Exam Tip

When you get calculation questions in the exam, remember to check what quantity they're actually asking you to find out, show all the steps of your working clearly and double-check every number that you type into your calculator.

Target AO3

3   A student is investigating osmosis. She takes three beakers and puts a different
concentration of sucrose solution into each one. Then she places a length of Visking
tubing (a partially permeable membrane) containing 0.5 M sucrose solution into
each beaker. She places a glass capillary tube in the Visking tubing so that the end
dips into the sucrose solution. A diagram of her experiment is shown in **Figure 1**.

Figure 1

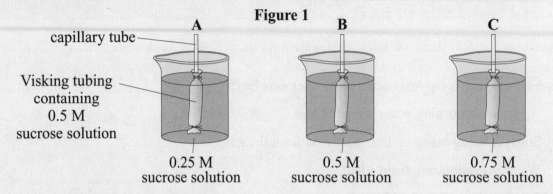

The student records the level of the sucrose solution in each beaker and each capillary tube
at the start of the experiment. She plans to record the level of the solution in each beaker
every 30 minutes for 8 hours.

3.1 Give **two** variables that the student should keep constant in this experiment.

....

....

[2]

3.2 Predict what will happen to the level of the solution in Beaker B after 1 hour.
Explain your answer.

....

....

....

[2]

3.3 Describe and explain what you would expect to happen to the level of solution in Beaker C
over the course of 8 hours.

....

....

....

....

....

[4]

[Total 8 marks]

Exam Tip

If you get a question in the exam where you need to explain the effects of osmosis, make sure you word your answer really
carefully. For example. remember to write about the movement of <u>water</u> molecules (not just molecules) and talk about
<u>water</u> concentration (not just 'the concentration') — these details will show the examiners you really know your stuff.

Active Transport

1 Sugar molecules can be absorbed from the gut into the blood by active transport.
Grade 4-6

1.1 Define active transport.

....

....

[1]

1.2 State how sugar molecules are used inside cells.

....

[1]

1.3 Which of these statements about active transport is correct? Tick **one** box.

☐ It is the way in which oxygen enters the blood from the lungs.

☐ It can only occur down a concentration gradient.

☐ It needs energy from respiration.

[1]

[Total 3 marks]

2 Plants absorb mineral ions from the soil by active transport.
Grade 6-7

2.1 Explain why plants need mineral ions.

....

[1]

2.2 Explain why plants are not able to rely on diffusion to absorb mineral ions from the soil.

....

....

[2]

2.3 State **two** ways in which active transport differs from diffusion.

....

....

[2]

2.4 Describe the function and structure of the root hair cells of a plant.
Include details of how the structure of the root hair cell helps it to carry out its function.

....

....

....

....

[3]

[Total 8 marks]

Topic 1 — Cell Biology

Exchange Surfaces

Place the following organisms in order according to their surface area to volume ratio. Number the boxes 1 to 4, with 1 being the smallest and 4 being the largest.

☐ Bacterium   ☐ Tiger   ☐ Domestic cat   ☐ Blue whale

1 Give **four** features of an effective gas exchange surface in an animal.   Grade 4-6

....

....

....

....

[Total 4 marks]

2 A student was investigating the effect of size on the uptake of substances by diffusion. He cut different sized cubes of agar containing universal indicator and placed them in beakers of acid. The student timed how long it took for the acid to diffuse through to the centre of each cube (and so completely change the colour of the agar).   Grade 7-9

Table 1 shows the relationship between the surface area and volume of the agar cubes.

Table 1

Cube size (cm)	Surface area (cm^2)	Volume (cm^3)	Simple ratio
2 × 2 × 2	24	8	3:1
3 × 3 × 3	**X**	**Y**	2:1
5 × 5 × 5	150	125	**Z** : 1

2.1 Calculate the values of X and Y in **Table 1**.

X = ... cm^2

Y = ... cm^3

[2]

2.2 Calculate the value of Z.

Z = ...

[1]

2.3 Predict which cube took the longest to change colour. Give **one** reason for your answer.

Cube ....

Reason ....

[1]

[Total 4 marks]

Exchanging Substances

1 **Figure 1** shows an alveolus in the lungs. (Grade 4-6)

Figure 1

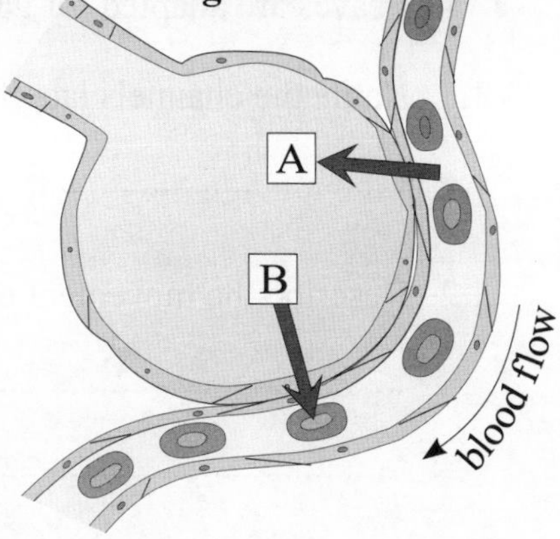

1.1 Name gases A and B.

A ....

B ....

[2]

1.2 By what process do these gases move across the membrane?

....

[1]

1.3 State which feature of the lungs gives them:

a short diffusion pathway ....

a large surface area ....

[2]

[Total 5 marks]

2 Emphysema is a disease that weakens and breaks down the walls of the alveoli. (Grade 6-7)

A person with emphysema may suffer from lower energy levels during physical exercise. Suggest and explain the cause of this symptom.

....

....

....

....

[Total 3 marks]

3 Describe and explain how the structure of the small intestine is adapted for absorbing the products of digestion. (Grade 6-7)

....

....

....

....

....

....

....

[Total 6 marks]

Exam Tip

It may seem obvious, but if you're asked to explain how the structure of something relates to its function, don't just dive straight in and rattle off what it looks like. First, focus on the function being asked about, then pick out the individual structures that help to do that function and for each structure, make sure you give a clear explanation of how it helps.

Topic 1 — Cell Biology

More on Exchanging Substances

1 Leaves are adapted for gas exchange. **Figure 1** shows the cross-section of a leaf.

Grade 4-6

1.1 Name the channels labelled X.

....
[1]

Figure 1

1.2 Describe the movement of gases into and out of the leaf.

....

....

....
[3]

air space

X

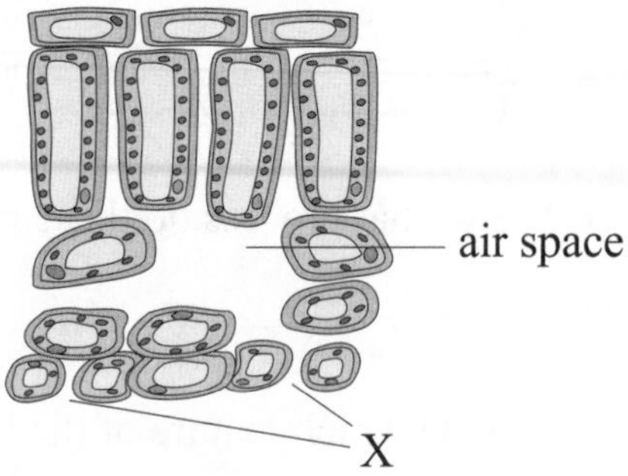

1.3 Suggest the purpose of the air spaces in the leaf.

....

....
[1]

[Total 5 marks]

2 **Figure 2** shows a diagram of a fish gill, which is a gas exchange surface.

Grade 6-7

2.1 How do gill filaments increase the
efficiency of the gas exchange surface?

....

....
[1]

Figure 2

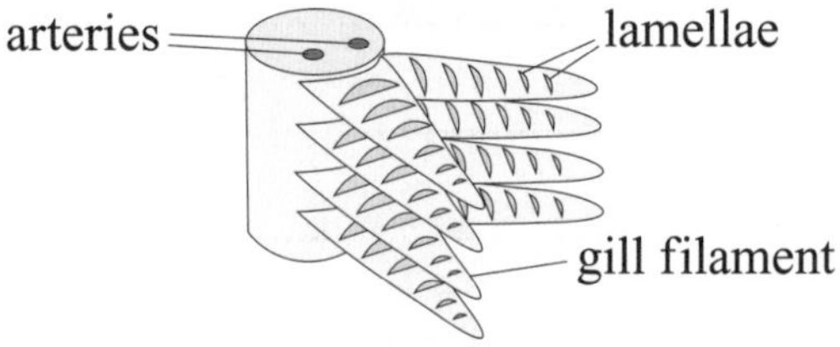

arteries

lamellae

gill filament

2.2 What is the purpose of the lamellae?

....
[1]

2.3 Describe one other feature of an efficient gas exchange surface that is present in **Figure 2**.

....
[1]

The number and length of gill filaments differ between types of fish.
2.4 Describe the differences in the gill filaments you would expect between
a fast-moving fish and a slow-moving fish.

....
[1]

2.5 Explain why you would expect to see these differences.

....

....
[2]

[Total 6 marks]

Topic 1 — Cell Biology

Cell Organisation

Number the boxes 1 to 4 to put the body components in order of size from smallest to largest, 1 being the smallest and 4 being the largest.

☐ **Organ system**   ☐ **Tissue**   ☐ **Cell**   ☐ **Organ**

1   The human digestive system is an example of an organ system.   (Grade 4-6)

1.1 **Figure 1** shows part of the digestive system.

Name organs X, Y and Z.

X: ....

Y: ....

Z: ....

[3]

Figure 1

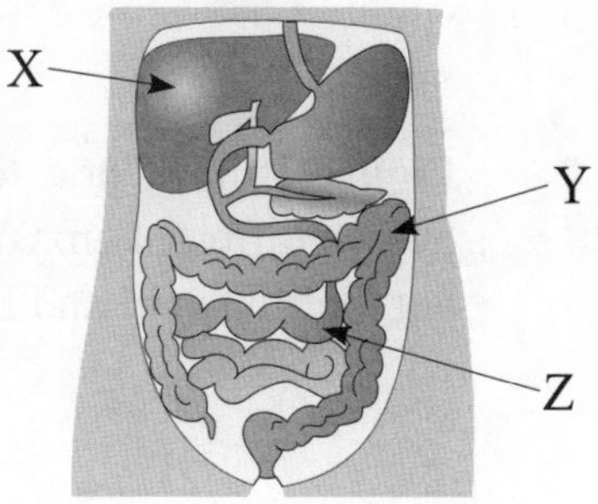

X →

→ Y

→ Z

1.2 What is meant by the term 'organ system'?

....

....

[1]

1.3 Organ systems contain multiple types of tissue.
What is a tissue?

....

....

[1]

1.4 What is the role of the digestive system?

....

[1]

1.5 The stomach is an organ that is part of the digestive system.
What is an organ?

....

....

[1]

[Total 7 marks]

Exam Tip

The examiners like to give you questions where you need to name or label things in a diagram. If they give you letters for different parts of the diagram, make sure that you write the right name next to the right letter and don't get them mixed up. Otherwise the examiners won't be able to give you the marks even though you clearly know your stuff.

Enzymes

1 Enzymes are biological catalysts. They increase the rate of biological reactions. **Figure 1** shows a typical enzyme.

Figure 1

1.1 Name the part of the enzyme labelled X.

....

[1]

1.2 Explain the function of part X in the action of an enzyme in a chemical reaction.

....

[1]

[Total 2 marks]

2 **Figure 2** shows how temperature affects the rate of a reaction when catalysed by two different enzymes. Enzyme A is from a species of bacteria found in a hot thermal vent and Enzyme B is from a species of bacteria found in soil.

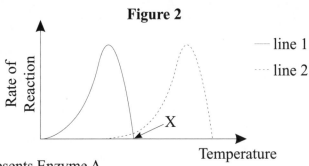

2.1 Suggest which line represents Enzyme A.

....

[1]

2.2 Explain your answer to 2.1.

....

....

....

[3]

2.3 Describe and explain what is happening at point X on the graph.

....

....

....

[4]

[Total 8 marks]

Exam Tip

Whenever you see the word 'suggest' in an exam question, that's your cue to gather all your knowledge on that topic and then apply it to a situation that you haven't seen before. So don't panic if you see an unfamiliar experiment or example — if the word 'suggest' is there just take what you already know and use it to have the best educated guess you can.

Topic 2 — Organisation

Investigating Enzymatic Reactions PRACTICAL

1 The enzyme amylase is involved in the breakdown of starch into simple sugars. (Grade 6-7)

A student investigated the effect of pH on the activity of amylase in starch solution. Amylase and starch solution were added to test tubes X, Y and Z. A different buffer solution was added to each test tube. Each buffer solution had a different pH value, as shown in **Figure 1**. Spotting tiles were prepared with a drop of iodine solution in each well. Iodine solution is a browny-orange colour but it turns blue-black in the presence of starch.

Figure 1

Test tube	pH
X	4
Y	6
Z	11

Every 30 seconds a drop of the solution from each of the test tubes was added to a separate well on a spotting tile. The resulting colour of the solution in the well was recorded as shown in **Figure 2**.

Figure 2

Time (s)	30	60	90	120	150
Tube X	Blue-black	Blue-black	Blue-black	Browny-orange	Browny-orange
Tube Y	Blue-black	Browny-orange	Browny-orange	Browny-orange	Browny-orange
Tube Z	Blue-black	Blue-black	Blue-black	Blue-black	Blue-black

1.1 State the pH at which the rate of reaction was greatest. Explain your answer.

....

....

....

[2]

1.2 Suggest an explanation for the results in tube **Z**.

....

....

[1]

1.3 In any experiment, it is important to control the variables that are not being tested. State how the student could control the temperature in the test tubes.

....

[1]

1.4 Give **two** other variables that should be controlled in this experiment.

1. ....

2. ....

[2]

1.5 The student repeated her experiment at pH 7 and got the same results as she got for her experiment at pH 6. Describe how she could improve her experiment to find whether the reaction is greatest at pH 6 or 7.

....

....

[1]

[Total 7 marks]

Topic 2 — Organisation

Enzymes and Digestion

The diagram on the right shows some of the organs in the digestive system. Lipases and proteases are examples of digestive enzymes.

Write an 'L' on the organs that produce lipases and write a 'P' on the organs that produce proteases.

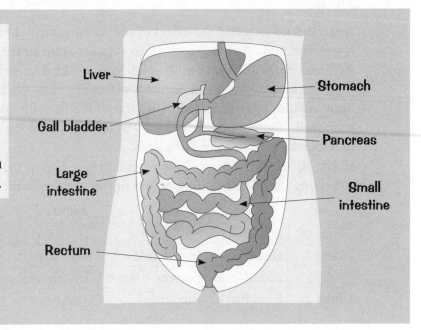

Liver

Stomach

Gall bladder

Pancreas

Large intestine

Small intestine

Rectum

1 Amylase is a digestive enzyme. Grade 4-6

1.1 Which group of digestive enzymes does amylase belong to?
Tick **one** box.

☐ Carbohydrases   ☐ Lipases   ☐ Proteases

[1]

1.2 What is the product of the reaction catalysed by amylase?
Tick **one** box.

☐ Sugars   ☐ Amino acids   ☐ Glycerol   ☐ Fatty acids

[1]

[Total 2 marks]

2 The process of digestion relies on the action of many different types of digestive enzyme. Grade 4-6

2.1 Describe the role of digestive enzymes in the process of digestion.

....

....

....

[2]

2.2 Give **two** ways in which the products of digestion can be used by the body.

....

....

[2]

[Total 4 marks]

Topic 2 — Organisation

3 Bile plays an important role in the digestive system. **Grade 6-7**

3.1 Name the organ where bile is produced and the organ where it is stored.

Produced .... Stored ....

[2]

3.2 Describe **two** functions of bile and for each one explain why it is important.

....

....

....

....

....

[4]

[Total 6 marks]

4* Different types of food molecule are broken down by different digestive enzymes. Using your knowledge of digestive enzymes and where they are produced in the body, fully outline the processes involved in the digestion of a meal containing carbohydrates, proteins and lipids. **Grade 7-9**

....

....

....

....

....

....

....

....

....

....

....

....

....

....

[Total 6 marks]

Topic 2 — Organisation

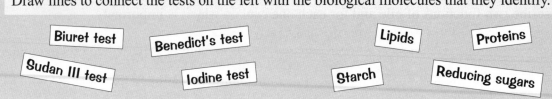

Food Tests

Warm-Up

Draw lines to connect the tests on the left with the biological molecules that they identify.

Biuret test   Benedict's test   Lipids   Proteins

Sudan III test   Iodine test   Starch   Reducing sugars

1* A student is analysing the nutrient content of egg whites.

Fully describe an investigation that the student could carry out to find out if protein is present in a sample of the egg whites.

....

....

....

....

....

....

....

[Total 6 marks]

2 A student was given test tubes containing the following glucose concentrations: 0 M, 0.02 M, 0.1 M, 1 M. The test tubes were not labelled and he was asked to perform tests to determine which test tube contained which glucose solution.

2.1 Describe the test he could carry out to try and distinguish between the glucose solutions.

....

....

....

[3]

2.2 **Table 1** shows the substance observed in the test tubes following his tests. Complete the table to show which glucose solution (0 M, 0.02 M, 0.1 M, 1 M) each test tube contained.

Table 1	Tube 1	Tube 2	Tube 3	Tube 4
substance observed	yellow precipitate	blue solution	red precipitate	green precipitate
glucose concentration (M)	....	....	....	....

[1]

[Total 4 marks]

The Lungs

Use the words on the right to correctly fill in the gaps in the passage.
You don't have to use every word, but each word can only be used once.

When you breathe in, air flows through a series of tubes, including the

trachea and the .... The .... are

where gas exchange takes place. Gas exchange ....

the blood and allows the removal of .... from the body.

oxygenates

arteries   alveoli

carbon dioxide

bronchi   oxygen

deoxygenates

1   **Figure 1** shows the human respiratory system. **Grade 4-6**

Figure 1

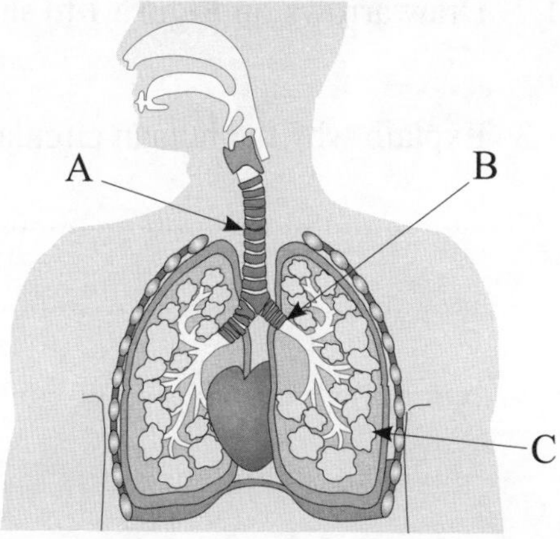

1.1   Name the parts labelled A, B and C in **Figure 1**.

A ....

B ....

C ....

[3]

Figure 2 shows a close-up of part C from **Figure 1**.

Figure 2

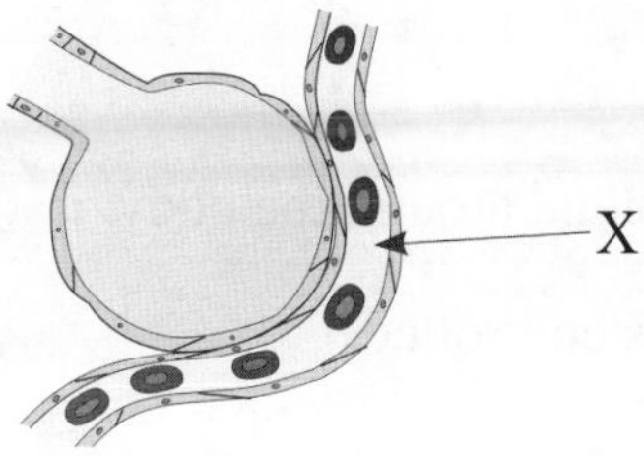

1.2   Name the structure labelled X in **Figure 2**.

....
[1]

1.3   Describe the role that structure X plays in gas exchange in the lungs.

....

....

....

....

....
[4]

[Total 8 marks]

Topic 2 — Organisation

Circulatory System — The Heart

1 Humans have a double circulatory system. The heart pumps blood around the body through a network of veins and arteries. **Figure 1** shows a diagram of the heart.

Grade **4-6**

1.1 Name the parts of the heart labelled X, Y and Z in **Figure 1**.

X ....

Y ....

Z ....

[3]

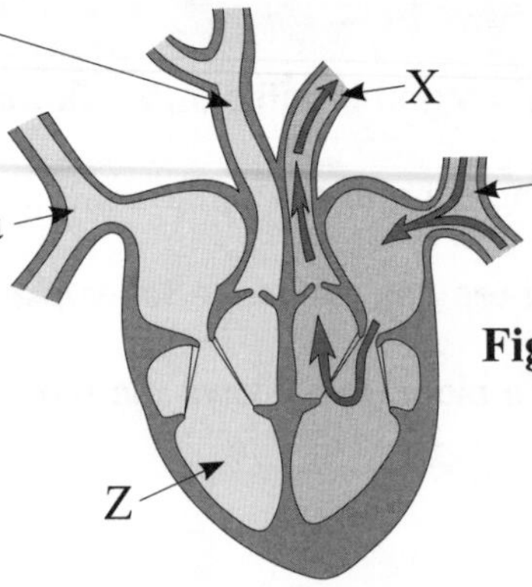

pulmonary artery

vena cava

X

Y

Z

Figure 1

1.2 Draw arrows on **Figure 1** to show the direction of blood flow through the right side of the heart.

[1]

1.3 Explain why the human circulatory system is described as a 'double circulatory system'.

....

....

....

....

....

[3]

[Total 7 marks]

2 The heart beats to circulate blood around the body. Grade **6-7**

2.1 Describe how the heartbeat is controlled.

....

....

[2]

2.2 Atrial fibrillation is a condition where the heartbeat is irregular. It is caused by problems with the heart's ability to control its own beat. Suggest how atrial fibrillation could be treated.

....

....

....

[2]

[Total 4 marks]

> **Exam Tip**
>
> Keep an eye out for different styles of questions where you're not given lines to write your answers on (like Q1.2 above). These sorts of questions can be easy to miss when you're under pressure, meaning you could be throwing away marks.

Circulatory System — Blood Vessels

1 Blood is carried around the body in blood vessels.
Different types of blood vessel perform different functions.

Figure 1 shows the three types of blood vessel.

Figure 1

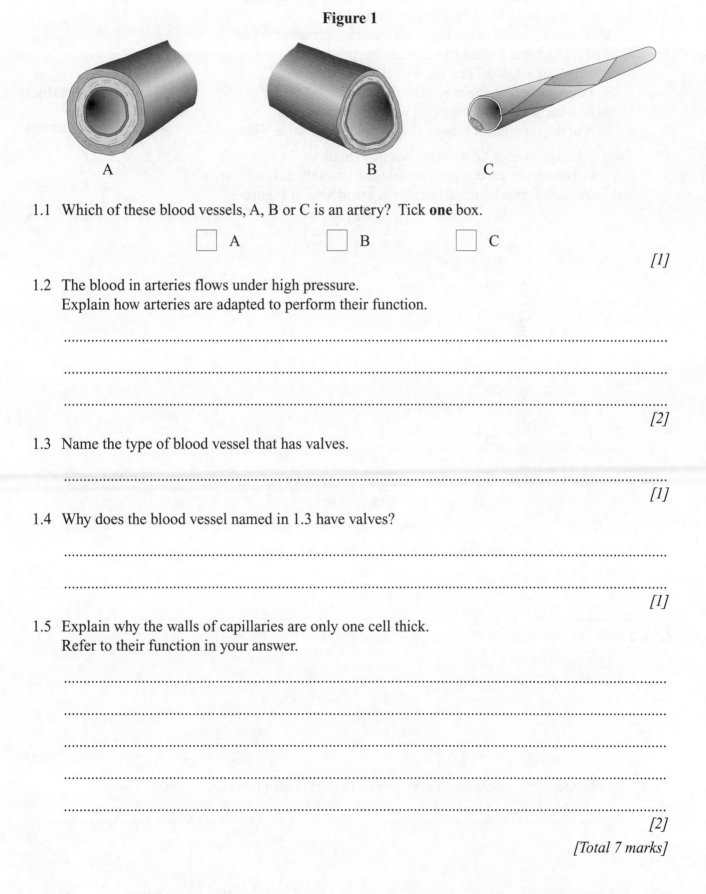

A   B   C

1.1 Which of these blood vessels, A, B or C is an artery? Tick **one** box.

☐ A   ☐ B   ☐ C

[1]

1.2 The blood in arteries flows under high pressure.
Explain how arteries are adapted to perform their function.

....

....

....

[2]

1.3 Name the type of blood vessel that has valves.

....

[1]

1.4 Why does the blood vessel named in 1.3 have valves?

....

....

[1]

1.5 Explain why the walls of capillaries are only one cell thick.
Refer to their function in your answer.

....

....

....

....

....

[2]

[Total 7 marks]

Topic 2 — Organisation

Target AO3

2   An investigation was carried out into the elasticity of arteries and veins.

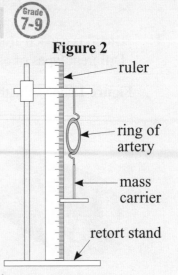

Figure 2

The experiment was set up as shown in **Figure 2**.
The method used was as follows:

1.   Cut a ring of tissue from an artery and attach it to the hook.
2.   Attach a mass carrier to the bottom of the ring.
3.   Measure the length of the ring with the mass carrier attached.
4.   Add a 10 g mass to the mass carrier.
5.   Measure the length of the ring with the mass attached,
     and then again with the mass removed.
6.   Repeat steps 4 and 5 with a 20 g mass, 30 g mass, etc.
7.   Repeat the experiment using a ring of vein of the same width.

The percentage change between the original length of the ring with
just the mass carrier attached and its length after each mass was removed
was calculated for each mass. The results are plotted in **Figure 3**.

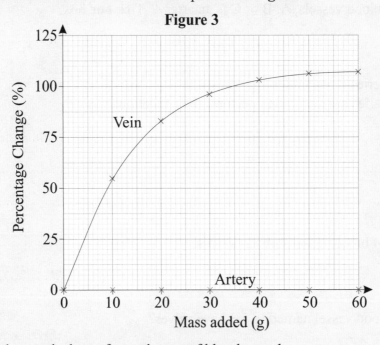

Figure 3

2.1   Describe what the graph shows for each type of blood vessel.

....

....

....

....

....

....

                                                                                                            [4]

2.2   Suggest **one** safety precaution that should be carried out for this experiment.

....

                                                                                                            [1]

                                                                                              [Total 5 marks]

Topic 2 — Organisation

Circulatory System — Blood

1 Blood is made up of several different components, including white blood cells, red blood cells and platelets.

Grade 7-9

1.1 Some diseases affect the body's ability to produce enough white blood cells. Suggest why people with these diseases are more likely to experience frequent infections.

....
[1]

1.2 Explain how white blood cells are adapted to perform their function.

....

....

....

....
[3]

1.3 Red blood cells carry oxygen from the lungs to other tissues in the body. Explain how red blood cells are adapted for their function.

....

....

....

....

....
[3]

The components of blood can be separated by spinning them at high speed. **Figure 1** shows a tube of blood that has been separated in this way.

Figure 1

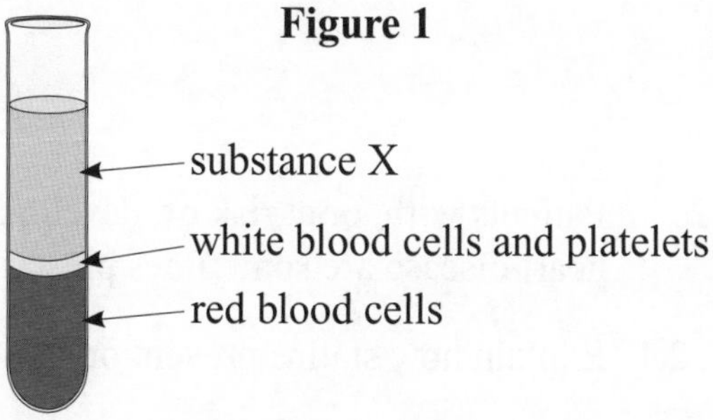

substance X

white blood cells and platelets

red blood cells

1.4 Identify the substance labelled X.

....
[1]

1.5 A scientist analysing the blood sample found that it had a lower than normal concentration of platelets. Describe the structure and function of platelets.

....

....
[2]

[Total 10 marks]

Exam Tip

Scientific terminology and key words are, well, key to use in science exams. You might find it easy to describe something in everyday language — but examiners often won't give you the marks unless you use the right scientific terminology.

Cardiovascular Disease

Use the correct words to fill in the gaps in the passage. Not all of them will be used.

pulmonary vein   blood vessels   asthma   aorta   coronary heart disease

coronary arteries   fatty acids   toxins   fatty material   cystic fibrosis

Cardiovascular disease is a term used to describe diseases of the ....

and heart. .... is an example of a cardiovascular disease.

It is caused by narrowing of the .... due to the build-up of

.... on the inside wall.

1   The coronary arteries surround the heart.
A patient has a blockage of fatty material in a coronary artery.

Grade 6-7

1.1   Explain why a blockage in the coronary arteries could cause damage to the patient's heart muscle.

....

....

[2]

1.2   Suggest and describe a method of treatment that a doctor might recommend to the patient.

....

....

....

[2]

[Total 4 marks]

2   Patients with, or at risk of, developing coronary heart disease are sometimes prescribed statins.

Grade 6-7

2.1   Explain how statins prevent or slow the progression of coronary heart disease.

....

....

....

[2]

2.2   A patient is offered statins. Suggest **one** reason why he may not wish to take them.

....

....

[1]

[Total 3 marks]

3 Doctors were assessing the heart of a patient recovering from a serious heart infection. (Grade 6-7)

3.1 They found that one of the valves in the heart had become leaky.
Suggest the effects this might have on blood flow through the heart and around the body.

....

....

....
[2]

3.2 Describe **one** other way that a valve might be faulty.

....
[1]

Surgeons decided to replace the faulty valve with a replacement biological valve.

3.3 What is a biological valve?

....
[1]

3.4 A mechanical valve is sometimes used in transplants instead of a biological valve.
What is a mechanical valve?

....
[1]

A second patient at the same hospital needed a heart transplant.
Heart transplants can use donor hearts or artificial hearts.

3.5 Artificial hearts are rarely used as a permanent fix.
Suggest when they are most likely to be used instead of a natural donor heart.

....

....

....
[2]

3.6 Suggest **one** advantage and **one** disadvantage of using a natural donor heart rather than an artificial heart in heart transplant operations.

Advantage ....

....

Disadvantage ....

....
[2]

[Total 9 marks]

Exam Tip

There are quite a few different ways to treat cardiovascular disease that could come up in your exam. As well as knowing what they are and how they work, make sure you can discuss the advantages and disadvantages of them too.

Topic 2 — Organisation

Health and Disease

1 Ill health is often caused by communicable and non-communicable diseases.

1.1 What is meant by the term 'communicable disease'?

....

....

[1]

1.2 List **two** factors other than disease that can cause ill health.

....

....

[2]

[Total 3 marks]

2 **Figure 1** and **Table 1** show the number of employees in five different rooms in a large office building who have had at least one common cold in the last 12 months.

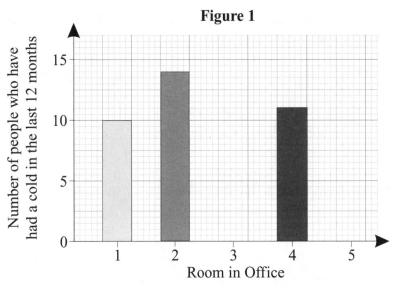

Table 1	Room 1	Room 2	Room 3	Room 4	Room 5	**Total**
Number of people who have had a cold in the last 12 months	10		12	11		**60**

2.1 Complete **Figure 1** and **Table 1**.

[4]

2.2 Some people have a defective immune system. Explain what effect this could have on the likelihood of a person contracting a communicable disease like the common cold.

....

....

....

[2]

[Total 6 marks]

Topic 2 — Organisation

Risk Factors for Non-Communicable Diseases

1 Substances in a person's environment can be risk factors for certain diseases. *Grade 4-6*

1.1 What is meant by a risk factor for a disease?

....

....

....
[1]

1.2 Other than substances in the environment, state **two** other types of risk factor.

....

....
[2]

1.3 Obesity is a risk factor for many different diseases.
Name **one** disease that obesity is a risk factor for.

....
[1]
[Total 4 marks]

2 A patient has been diagnosed with cardiovascular disease. *Grade 4-6*

2.1 Give **two** risk factors that might have contributed to her developing cardiovascular disease.

....

....
[2]

2.2 Suggest **two** reasons why non-communicable diseases can be financially costly.

....

....

....

....
[2]
[Total 4 marks]

Exam Tip

Remember that risk factors are identified by scientists looking for correlations in data, and they don't always directly cause a disease. Sometimes, they are just related to another factor that does. It's rarely a single risk factor that leads to someone developing a disease — diseases are often caused when multiple risk factors interact with each other.

Target AO3

3   **Figures 1** and **2** show the prevalence of adult obesity in England and the number of people diagnosed with diabetes in England, respectively, between 2012 and 2018.

Figure 1

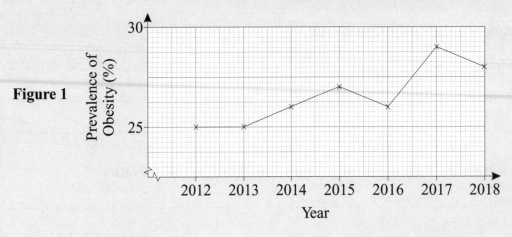

Figure 2

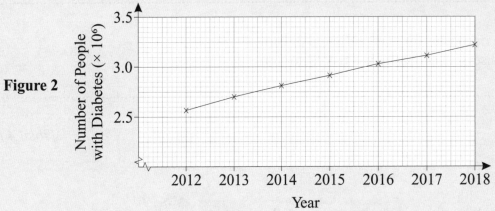

3.1   Describe the trend shown in **Figure 2**.

....

....

[1]

3.2* A student says: "the increasing rate of obesity has caused the rate of diabetes to increase". Evaluate the student's statement using the data shown in **Figures 1** and **2**.

....

....

....

....

....

....

....

....

[4]

[Total 5 marks]

Cancer

Warm-Up

Tumours can be benign or malignant. Draw lines to match the types of tumour on the left with each characteristic on the right that applies to them.

Malignant Tumours

Are cancerous

Are not cancerous

Benign Tumours

Can invade neighbouring tissues

1 Some types of tumour are cancerous. **Grade 4-6**

1.1 What do tumours result from?
Tick **one** box.

☐ Rapid cell death

☐ Slow cell division

☐ Lack of cell division

☐ Uncontrolled cell division

[1]

1.2 There are many known lifestyle-related risk factors for cancer. However, not all risk factors for cancer are related to lifestyle. Give **one** other type of risk factor for cancer.

....
[1]

[Total 2 marks]

2 Doctors found a tumour in the left lung of a patient.
They were concerned that the patient was at risk of developing secondary tumours. **Grade 6-7**

2.1 Was the tumour in the patient's lung malignant or benign?

....
[1]

2.2 Explain how a secondary tumour forms.

....

....

....
[2]

[Total 3 marks]

 ☐ ☐ ☐

Plant Cell Organisation

1   The roots, stem and leaves are involved in the transport of substances around a plant.   (Grade 4-6)

1.1   What do the roots, stem and leaves of a plant form? Tick **one** box.

☐ A tissue   ☐ An organ system   ☐ An organ   ☐ A tissue system

[1]

1.2   Name **two** substances that are transported around a plant in the xylem.

....

[2]

[Total 3 marks]

2   Plants have many types of tissue, including meristem tissue.   (Grade 4-6)

2.1   Name **two** sites in a plant where you would find meristem tissue.

....

....

[2]

2.2   Give **one** reason why meristem tissue is important throughout the life of the plant.

....

[1]

[Total 3 marks]

3   **Figure 1** shows a transverse section of a leaf.   (Grade 6-7)

Figure 1

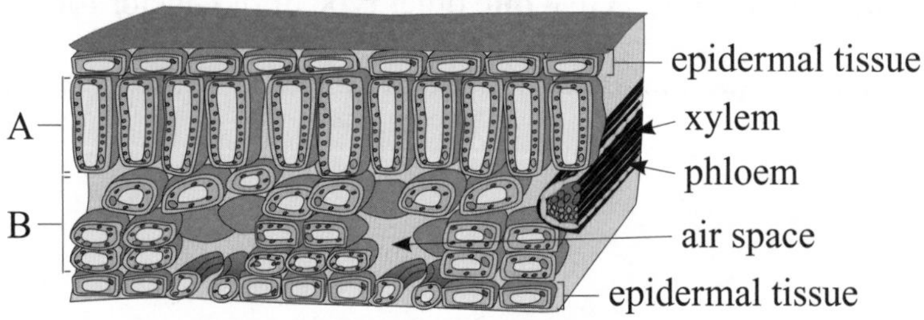

epidermal tissue
xylem
phloem
air space
epidermal tissue
A
B

3.1   Name the tissues labelled A and B.

A ....   B ....

[2]

3.2   Explain how the tissue labelled A is adapted for the function of photosynthesis.

....

....

....

[2]

3.3   What is the function of the air spaces?

....

[1]

[Total 5 marks]

Topic 2 — Organisation

Transpiration and Translocation

Use the words below to correctly fill in the gaps in the passage.
You don't have to use every word, but each word can only be used once.

| leaves | phloem | translocation | mineral ions | condensation | evaporation |
| roots | perspiration | xylem | transpiration | sugars | guard cells | stem |

The process by which water is lost from a plant is called ....

It is caused by the .... and diffusion of water from a plant's surface,

most often from the .... Another process, called ....,

is the transport of .... from where they're made in the leaves to the rest

of the plant via the .... vessels.

1* Describe how xylem tissue and phloem tissue work to:
- supply water and mineral ions to all parts of a plant,
- transport dissolved sugars around a plant.

Include details of the **structure** and **function** of the tissues involved.

Grade
7-9

....

....

....

....

....

....

....

....

....

....

....

....

[Total 6 marks]

Transpiration and Stomata

1   **Figure 1** is a drawing of a magnified image of part of the surface of a leaf

Figure 1

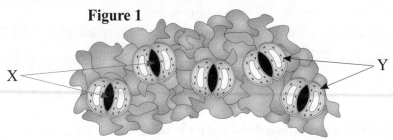

1.1   Name the structures labelled X and the cells labelled Y in **Figure 1**.

X ....   Y ....

[2]

1.2   What is the function of the cells labelled Y?

....

....

....

[2]

[Total 4 marks]

2   **Table 1** shows the diameter of ten stomata from each of two leaves, A and B.

Table 1

Diameter of stomata (μm)	
Leaf A	Leaf B
25.2, 20.1, 18.7, 17.9, 19.1, 19.3, 22.0, 23.1, 21.8, 20.3	14.7, 12.8, 14.1, 13.2, 12.9, 11.9, 12.1, 13.4, 10.9, 11.7

2.1   Calculate the mean width of the stomata for each leaf.

Leaf A = ... μm   Leaf B = ... μm

[2]

2.2   Leaves A and B are from the same species. Which leaf do you think had its stomatal measurements taken in lower light intensity?

....

[1]

2.3   Explain your answer to 2.2.

....

....

....

[2]

[Total 5 marks]

3 An investigation was carried out to assess the rate of water uptake by a plant over a 16-hour period.

A potometer was set up and readings were taken every two hours between 00:00 and 16:00.
The rate in cm³/hour was calculated for each two-hour period. The results are shown in **Table 2**.

Table 2

Time of day	00:00	02:00	04:00	06:00	08:00	10:00	12:00	14:00	16:00
Rate of water uptake (cm³/hour)	2.6	1.0	1.6	2.0	3.8	6.2	8.0	10.2	7.6

3.1 Complete **Figure 2** using the data displayed in **Table 2**.
   - Select a suitable scale and label for the y-axis
   - Plot the rate of water uptake in cm³/hour for all the times given in **Table 2**
   - Join the points with straight lines

Figure 2

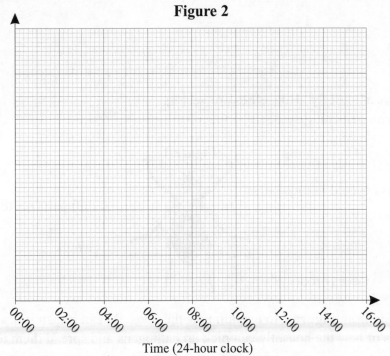

Time (24-hour clock)

[4]

3.2 Use the graph to estimate the rate of water uptake at 09:00.

....

[1]

3.3 How much did the rate of water uptake increase between 06:00 and 11:00?

....

[1]

3.4 Suggest **two** environmental changes that could have caused the change in water uptake between 06:00 and 14:00.

....

....

[2]

[Total 8 marks]

Exam Tip

Make sure you look at the scales on graphs very carefully. Read the numbers written next to the big squares and then carefully work out how much each small square is worth. For example, it's easy to assume they're worth 0.1 instead of 0.2.

Topic 2 — Organisation

Communicable Disease

1   Viruses and bacteria can both reproduce inside the human body.   (Grade 4-6)

1.1   Which of the following sentences is correct? Tick **one** box.

◻ Both bacteria and viruses can reproduce quickly in the body.

◻ Bacteria reproduce quickly in the body, but viruses reproduce slowly.

◻ Viruses reproduce quickly in the body, but bacteria reproduce slowly.

◻ Both bacteria and viruses reproduce slowly in the body.

[1]

1.2   Viruses reproduce inside cells. Describe what problem this can cause for the cells.

....

[1]

[Total 2 marks]

2*   **Figure 1** shows a housefly. Houseflies are vectors because they can transmit disease to humans.   (Grade 7-9)

Figure 1

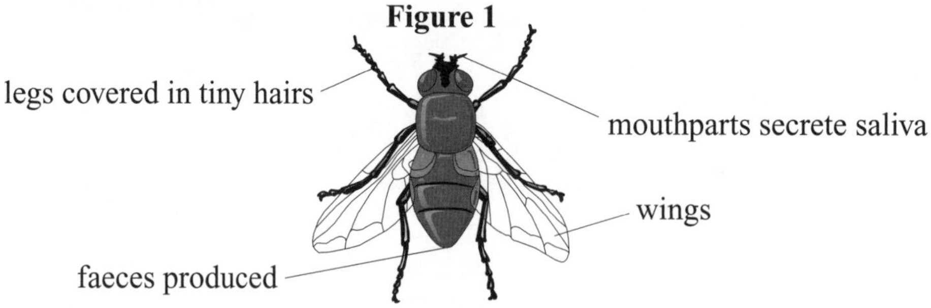

legs covered in tiny hairs

mouthparts secrete saliva

wings

faeces produced

Use information from **Figure 1** to explain how the housefly can transmit disease to humans. Include details of how the housefly can pick up pathogens and spread them to humans.

....

....

....

....

....

....

....

....

[Total 6 marks]

Exam Tip

It might not feel like it, but the examiners really aren't trying to confuse you. Every word in a question is there for a reason. So, for example, if the question tells you to 'include details' of something, you need to do that to get the marks.

Viral, Fungal and Protist Diseases

Fill in the gaps in the passage about malaria. Use the words on the left.
Not all of the words will be used.

protist breeding

vectors

fever fungi

virus bacterium

Malaria is caused by a .... Mosquitoes are the

.... that carry the malaria pathogen to humans.

Malaria causes repeating episodes of .... The spread of

malaria can be reduced by stopping the mosquitoes from ....

1 Measles is a highly infectious disease. *Grade 4-6*

1.1 What type of pathogen causes measles? Tick **one** box.

☐ bacterium ☐ virus ☐ protist ☐ fungus

[1]

1.2 A person suffering from measles travels to work by train. Explain how, 10 days later, other people who were on the same train may also be suffering from measles.

....

....

....

[3]

1.3 Measles can be fatal if there are complications.
What can be done to prevent someone from developing measles?

....

[1]

[Total 5 marks]

2 A virus called HIV causes a disease known as AIDS. *Grade 4-6*

2.1 What type of drug can be used to control HIV?

....

[1]

2.2 What system in the body does HIV attack?

....

[1]

2.3 State **two** ways in which HIV can be spread.

....

....

[2]

[Total 4 marks]

3 The tobacco mosaic virus (TMV) is a widespread plant pathogen affecting many species of plants.

(Grade 6-7)

3.1 Name **one** species of plant that is often attacked by the tobacco mosaic virus.

....

[1]

3.2 Describe the appearance of a plant with TMV.

....

[1]

3.3 Outline why a plant affected by TMV cannot grow properly.

....

....

[1]

3.4 **Table 1** shows the mean diameter and mass of fruits from 100 healthy plants and 100 plants infected with TMV.

Table 1

	Healthy plants	Plants with TMV
Mean diameter of fruit (mm)	50	35
Mean mass of fruit (g)	95	65

Describe the effect of TMV on the diameter and mass of fruit produced in the infected plants compared to the healthy plants.

....

....

....

[2]

[Total 5 marks]

4 Rose black spot is a disease that can affect rose plants.

(Grade 6-7)

4.1 Describe the appearance of leaves that are infected with rose black spot and state what happens to these leaves.

....

....

[3]

4.2 A gardener notices that one of her rose plants is infected with rose black spot.
She is worried about the rest of her rose plants becoming infected with the fungus.
Why are the other rose plants in her garden at risk from being infected with the disease?

....

[1]

4.3 Rose black spot can be treated by removing and destroying the infected leaves and treating the rest of the plant with a fungicide. Suggest why it is important to destroy the removed leaves.

....

....

[1]

[Total 5 marks]

Bacterial Diseases and Preventing Disease

1   *Salmonella* food poisoning in humans is caused by a bacterium.   *Grade 4-6*

1.1   List **two** symptoms of *Salmonella* food poisoning.

....

....

[2]

1.2   What does the *Salmonella* bacterium produce that causes these symptoms?

....

[1]

1.3   In the UK, poultry are vaccinated against the bacterium that causes food poisoning.
Explain why it is necessary to vaccinate poultry.

....

....

....

[2]

1.4   Suggest **one** way that a person suffering from *Salmonella* food poisoning can prevent passing the disease on to someone else.

....

[1]

[Total 6 marks]

2   Gonorrhoea is a disease that can affect both men and women.   *Grade 4-6*

2.1   How is gonorrhoea spread from person to person?

....

[1]

2.2   State **two** symptoms of the disease in women.

....

....

[2]

2.3   Name the antibiotic that was originally used to treat people infected with gonorrhoea.

....

[1]

2.4   Name **one** barrier method of contraception that prevents the spread of gonorrhoea.

....

[1]

[Total 5 marks]

Exam Tip

You'll often get questions that specify how many things you need to include in your answer. Double-check you've written the right number of things before you move on — there's no way you can get full marks if you don't write enough.

Fighting Disease

1 The body has many features that it can use to protect itself against pathogens. **Grade 4-6**

1.1 Describe how the skin helps to defend the body against pathogens.

....

....
[2]

1.2 How do structures in the nose help to defend the body against the entry of pathogens?

....

....
[1]
[Total 3 marks]

2* Describe how the human body works to defend itself against pathogens that have entered the body. Include details of the body's defences and the role of the immune system. **Grade 6-7**

....

....

....

....

....

....

....

....

....

....

....
[Total 6 marks]

Exam Tip

Think carefully about 6 mark questions like the one on this page. Don't just start scribbling everything you know about the topic. Stop and think first — work out what the question is wanting you to write about, and then make sure you write enough points to bag yourself as many marks as possible. Good job you've got some practice on this page.

Topic 3 — Infection and Response

Fighting Disease — Vaccination

1 Children are often vaccinated against measles. (Grade 4-6)

1.1 What is injected into the body during a vaccination?

....

[1]

1.2 Describe what happens when a vaccine is injected into the body. Tick **one** box.

☐ Red blood cells are stimulated to produce antibodies.

☐ White blood cells are stimulated to produce antibiotics.

☐ Red blood cells are stimulated to produce antibiotics.

☐ White blood cells are stimulated to produce antibodies.

[1]

[Total 2 marks]

2 People can be vaccinated against a large number of diseases. (Grade 6-7)

2.1 If the mumps pathogen enters the body of someone who has had the mumps vaccination, why would they be unlikely to become ill with mumps?

....

[1]

2.2 A large proportion of a population is vaccinated against a particular pathogen. Suggest why the spread of the pathogen will be very much reduced.

....

....

....

[2]

[Total 3 marks]

3 When visiting some other countries, it is recommended that travellers are vaccinated against some of the serious diseases found in those countries. (Grade 7-9)

3.1 If a traveller planned to visit a country where there had been a recent outbreak of the communicable disease cholera, they might get vaccinated against cholera before they travelled. Give **two** reasons why this would be beneficial.

....

....

[2]

3.2 Some countries insist that travellers have had particular vaccinations before they are allowed to enter the country. Suggest why.

....

[1]

[Total 3 marks]

Topic 3 — Infection and Response

Fighting Disease — Drugs

1 There are many different types of drugs with different functions. (Grade 6-7)

1.1 Explain why it is difficult to develop drugs to kill viruses.

....

....

[2]

1.2 Many people suffer from sore throats caused by bacteria. Other than an antibiotic, name a type of drug that could be used to ease the symptoms of the infection.

....

[1]

1.3 Explain why the type of drug named in 1.2 would not be able to cure the bacterial infection.

....

[1]

[Total 4 marks]

2 A hospital records the number of cases of infections that are caused by antibiotic-resistant bacteria each year. The figures for three years are shown in **Table 1**. (Grade 6-7)

Table 1

Year	2013	2014	2015
No. of infections	84	102	153

2.1 What is meant by antibiotic-resistant bacteria?

....

....

[1]

2.2 Describe the trend shown in **Table 1**.

....

....

[1]

2.3 Use **Table 1** to calculate the percentage change in antibiotic-resistant infections between 2013 and 2015.

.... %

[2]

[Total 4 marks]

Exam Tip

When you're answering an exam question about drugs and disease, think very carefully about whether the drug kills the pathogens causing the disease (and so cures it), or whether it just helps to make the symptoms of the disease better.

Topic 3 — Infection and Response

Developing Drugs

1 New drugs have to be tested and trialled before they can be used. Grade 4-6

1.1 List **three** things drugs must be tested for, to ensure they are safe and effective.

....

....

....

[3]

1.2 Which of the following is preclinical testing carried out on? Tick **one** box.

☐ healthy human volunteers   ☐ patients in a hospital

☐ cells, tissues and dead animals   ☐ cells, tissues and live animals

[1]

[Total 4 marks]

2 Clinical trials are always carried out on healthy volunteers before patients. Grade 7-9

2.1 Suggest why very low doses of the drug are given at the start of clinical trials.

....

[1]

2.2 Clinical trials are often double-blind. Explain what would happen in a double-blind clinical trial.

....

....

....

[3]

2.3 Suggest why clinical trials are carried out using a double-blind method.

....

....

[1]

The final results of clinical trials cannot be published until they have been checked
by other scientists. Such checking is often referred to as peer review.

2.4 Suggest why peer review is important in these trials.

....

[1]

2.5 Suggest why it is important that the scientists who carry out the peer review have
no links to the people who carried out the original trials.

....

....

[2]

[Total 8 marks]

 ☐   ☐   ☐

Monoclonal Antibodies

Circle the correct underlined words below, so that each sentence is correct.

Monoclonal antibodies are made by <u>lymphocytes</u>/<u>pathogens</u>. They can be used to locate particular protein antigens in a blood sample by being bound to a <u>fluorescent dye</u>/<u>drug</u>. The monoclonal antibodies will <u>attach to</u>/<u>dye</u> the protein antigens and can be detected.

1 **Figure 1** shows a monoclonal antibody. It will attach to a particular antigen.

Figure 1

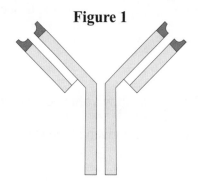

1.1 On **Figure 1**, circle where the antibody will bind to the antigen.

[1]

Figure 2 shows some antigens.

Figure 2

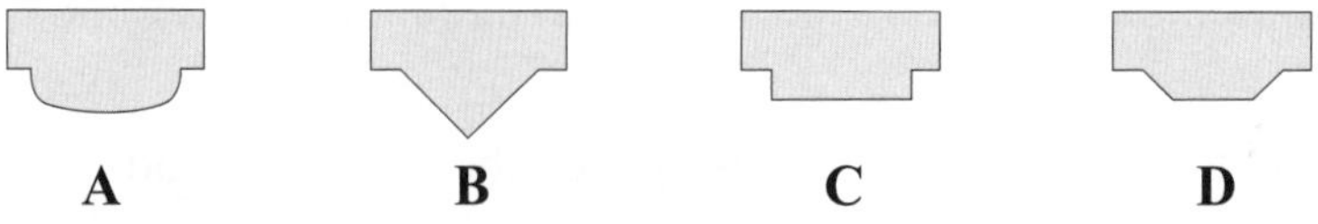

| A | B | C | D |

1.2 Which antigen will the antibody in **Figure 1** attach to? Tick **one** box.

☐ Antigen **A**   ☐ Antigen **B**   ☐ Antigen **C**   ☐ Antigen **D**

[1]
[Total 2 marks]

2 Monoclonal antibodies have lots of uses.

What are monoclonal antibodies?

....

....

....

[Total 2 marks]

3 Monoclonal antibodies can be used to treat cancer. Grade 6-7

3.1 Explain how monoclonal antibodies can be used to treat cancer.

....

....

....

....

....

[4]

3.2 When monoclonal antibodies were first discovered, it was thought that they would be used more widely in medical treatments than they actually are. Explain why this has not been the case.

....

[1]

3.3 Treating cancer is just one use of monoclonal antibodies.
Give **two** more uses of monoclonal antibodies.

....

....

[2]

[Total 7 marks]

4* Monoclonal antibodies are engineered by scientists. Grade 7-9

Describe the process of making monoclonal antibodies.

....

....

....

....

....

....

....

....

....

....

....

....

[Total 6 marks]

Exam Tip

Make sure you know what an exam question is looking for. If a question asks you to 'describe' something, you'll need to remember some facts about that thing or process and write them down as clearly as you can. But if a question asks you to 'explain' something, you'll need to give reasons for why or how that thing happens, or make something really clear.

Topic 3 — Infection and Response

Plant Diseases and Defences

1 Plants can be infected by a range of different types of pathogens. *Grade 4-6*

1.1 Name a virus that plants can be infected with.

....

[1]

1.2 Name a fungus that can cause disease in plants.

....

[1]

1.3 Insects can also affect plants. Name **one** insect that can cause damage to plants.

....

[1]

[Total 3 marks]

2 A gardener notices that one of his plants has spots on its leaves. *Grade 6-7*
He thinks that this might be a sign of a disease.

2.1 List **four** other signs that a plant has a disease.

....

....

....

[4]

2.2 The gardener tries using a gardening manual to identify the disease.
Suggest **two** other ways that the gardener could identify the disease that has infected his plant.

....

....

[2]

2.3 A gardener counts that he has 42 plants in his garden.
Table 1 shows the number of those plants infected by a pathogen.

Table 1

	Infected by fungus	Infected by virus
No. of plants	12	6

Calculate the percentage of plants that have a viral infection.

.... %

[2]

[Total 8 marks]

Exam Tip

If you're given a table in a question, make sure you have a good old look at it. Take a few moments to read the titles of the columns and rows, and figure out what the numbers inside it all mean. It'll help you figure out what to do next.

Topic 3 — Infection and Response

3   Plants have many ways of defending themselves.   (Grade 6-7)

3.1   Suggest how having cellulose cell walls protects a plant from microorganisms.

....

[1]

3.2   Give **two** types of chemical that plants can produce for defence.
For each type of chemical, explain how it helps the plant to survive.

....

....

....

....

[4]

3.3   State **two** types of mechanical adaptation that help plants to protect themselves.
For each one, explain how it works.

....

....

....

....

[4]

[Total 9 marks]

4   Plants need a range of minerals ions in order to remain healthy.   (Grade 6-7)

4.1   A plant has stunted growth. Suggest what mineral it is deficient in.

....

[1]

4.2   Explain why a deficiency in the mineral you named in 4.1 causes stunted growth in plants.

....

....

[2]

4.3   Other than the mineral you named in 4.1, name another mineral ion that plants require for
healthy growth.

....

[1]

4.4   Explain how a deficiency in the ion you named in 4.3 affects a plant.

....

....

....

[2]

[Total 6 marks]

Target AO3

5   A student investigated how mineral ion deficiencies affect plant growth. He planted 20 radish seedlings in a growth medium containing a complete supply of minerals. Then he planted 20 more in a growth medium deficient in nitrate and 20 in a growth medium deficient in magnesium. He left the plants to grow for 17 days.

At the end of the investigation, the student measured the total dry mass of each group of plants. His results are shown in **Figure 1**.

Figure 1

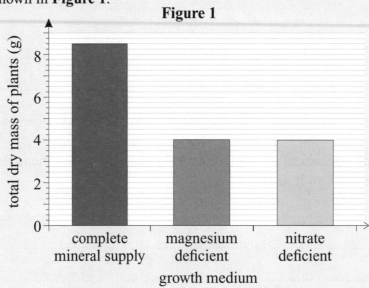

5.1 The student says, "The seedlings that had a complete mineral supply grew twice as well as the ones deficient in nitrate or magnesium."

Explain how the data shown in **Figure 1** supports the student's conclusion.

....

....

....

....

[3]

5.2 Identify the dependent and independent variables in the student's experiment.

....

....

[2]

5.3 The student reads that phosphate is another important nutrient for plant growth. He thinks that seedlings that don't get enough phosphate might have smaller leaves than normal seedlings. Outline an experiment he could do to test his hypothesis.

....

....

....

....

[3]

[Total 8 marks]

Topic 3 — Infection and Response

Target AO3

6   A scientist has a pear tree. She notices that some of the pears on the tree have soft, brown patches on them. She decides to perform an experiment to work out if the damage is being caused by a plant pathogen. Her method is shown below.

> Method
> 1) Pick a pear with a brown patch on it and seal it in a plastic bag. Wash your hands.
> 2) Pick a healthy pear from the tree and wash it.
> 3) Sterilise a metal skewer. Use it to make two holes on opposite sides of the healthy pear.
> 4) Sterilise the skewer again. Open the plastic bag and dip the skewer into the brown patch on the unhealthy pear. Reseal the bag.
> 5) Insert the skewer into one of the holes you made in the healthy pear.
> 6) Put the healthy pear in a clean plastic tub. Keep it at room temperature for two weeks.

6.1 Look at **step 3**. Suggest why it is necessary to sterilise the skewer before it is used.

....

....

[1]

6.2 Suggest why two holes are made in the healthy pear, even though material from the unhealthy pear is only added to one of them.

....

....

[1]

6.3 Describe what the scientist should observe about the healthy pear after two weeks if the soft, brown patches are caused by a plant pathogen.

....

....

....

[2]

6.4 At the end of the experiment, the scientist looks at the pear and concludes that the patches were caused by a plant pathogen. Describe what she should do to show that her results are reproducible.

....

....

[1]

[Total 5 marks]

Exam Tip

Don't panic if you get asked questions in an exam about an experiment that you haven't come across before. You won't be asked anything that you can't figure out based on your knowledge of the subject and of the practical work that you've done during the course. Of course, that does mean you'll actually have to pay attention in practicals...

Topic 3 — Infection and Response

Topic 4 — Bioenergetics

Photosynthesis and Limiting Factors

1 Photosynthesis is where energy is transferred to plants and used to make glucose. **Grade 4-6**

1.1 What is the source of energy for photosynthesis?

....

[1]

1.2 Complete the following word equation for photosynthesis.

.... + water → glucose + ...

[2]

Plants use the glucose they produce in lots of different ways, including to make a substance to strengthen cell walls.

1.3 Name the substance that plants use to strengthen cell walls.

....

[1]

1.4 Give **two** other ways that plants use the glucose produced during photosynthesis.

....

....

....

[2]

[Total 6 marks]

2 Photosynthesis is an endothermic reaction. Various factors affect its rate. **Grade 6-7**

2.1 Explain what is meant by an endothermic reaction.

....

[1]

2.2 Which of the following factors does not affect the rate of photosynthesis? Tick **one** box.

☐ carbon dioxide concentration   ☐ nitrate concentration   ☐ light intensity   ☐ temperature

[1]

2.3 A lack of magnesium can cause chloroplasts not to make enough chlorophyll. Explain what effect this would have on the rate of photosynthesis of a plant.

....

....

[2]

[Total 4 marks]

Exam Tip

With multiple choice questions, it's a good idea to read them over a couple of times before choosing your answer. Check that you've looked at all the options and that you've understood the question properly. For example, does the question ask for the thing or <u>not</u> the thing (like in Q2.2 above)? Don't make silly mistakes by rushing into your answer.

The Rate of Photosynthesis

Choose from the words below to complete the sentences explaining how temperature affects the rate of photosynthesis, as shown in the graph. Some words may not be used at all.

quickly   low   high   slowly   damaged   replaced

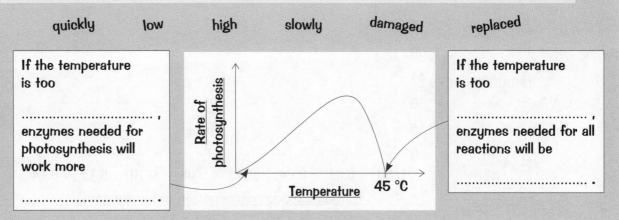

If the temperature is too

.... ,

enzymes needed for photosynthesis will work more

....

If the temperature is too

.... ,

enzymes needed for all reactions will be

....

1   **Figure 1** shows a greenhouse. Greenhouses are used to create the ideal conditions for photosynthesis.

Figure 1

1.1 Suggest **two** ways that a farmer could improve the conditions for photosynthesis in a greenhouse. For each of the ways, explain how it affects the rate of photosynthesis.

Improvement ....

Explanation ....

....

Improvement ....

Explanation ....

....

[4]

1.2 Creating the ideal conditions in a greenhouse costs money. Explain why it may still be beneficial for the farmer to do this.

....

....

[2]

[Total 6 marks]

Topic 4 — Bioenergetics

2 A student carried out an experiment to investigate the effect of changing the concentration of carbon dioxide on the rate of photosynthesis in a green plant. The results were plotted on the graph shown in **Figure 2**.

Figure 2

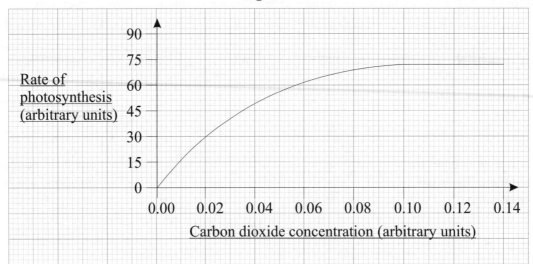

2.1 Describe the trend shown in the graph.

....

....

....

[2]

2.2 At a certain point, the CO_2 concentration is no longer limiting the rate of photosynthesis. Suggest **two** factors that could be limiting the rate at this point.

....

....

[2]

2.3 In the space below, sketch a graph to show how light intensity affects the rate of photosynthesis.

[2]

[Total 6 marks]

Exam Tip

If a question asks you to 'sketch' a graph, it doesn't mean it needs to be a work of art. It just means that you've got to draw some axes (with labels, of course) and then draw approximately what the shape of the graph would look like.

Topic 4 — Bioenergetics

PRACTICAL

3   A student was investigating the effect of light intensity on the rate of
photosynthesis in a water plant. She set up the experiment as shown in **Figure 3**.

Figure 3

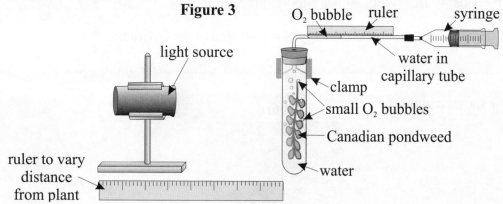

3.1 Predict what will happen to the volume of gas produced
when the light is moved closer to the pondweed.

....

[1]

3.2 The formula $1/distance^2$ can be used as a measure of light intensity. It's called the inverse
square law. Use the inverse square law to calculate the light intensity when the lamp is 20 cm
from the pondweed.

light intensity = ... arbitrary units

[2]

3.3* Suggest how the student could adapt the experiment shown in **Figure 3**
to investigate the effect of temperature on the rate of photosynthesis.
Include details of the variables that should be controlled.

....

....

....

....

....

....

....

....

[6]

[Total 9 marks]

Exam Tip

There's a lot to learn about limiting factors and the rate of photosynthesis. It's a good idea to practise drawing the
graphs to show the effect of light intensity, carbon dioxide concentration and temperature on the rate of photosynthesis.
You should also make sure you're able to interpret the graphs too, including those with more than one factor involved.

 ☐   ☐   ☐

Topic 4 — Bioenergetics

Respiration and Metabolism

1   Respiration is a reaction carried out by all living organisms.
It transfers energy from an organism's food to their cells.

Grade
6-7

1.1 Name the type of reaction where energy is transferred to the environment.

....

[1]

Figure 1 shows a gull.

Figure 1

1.2 Give **three** examples of how a gull uses the energy transferred by respiration.

....

....

....

[3]

[Total 4 marks]

2   Metabolism is the sum of all of the reactions that happen in a cell
or the body. Metabolism includes reactions that make molecules.

Grade
6-7

2.1 Some metabolic reactions involve using glucose molecules to make other molecules.
Name a molecule made from glucose in plants, and a molecule made from glucose in animals.

Plants ....

Animals ....

[2]

2.2 Describe the components of a lipid molecule.

....

....

[2]

2.3 Briefly describe how protein molecules are formed.

....

....

[2]

2.4 Metabolism also involves breaking down molecules.
What is excess protein broken down to produce?

....

[1]

[Total 7 marks]

Topic 4 — Bioenergetics

Target AO3

3   A student is investigating respiration in germinating peas. She predicts that germinating peas will respire, and so will release energy as heat.

The student sets up her experiment as shown in **Figure 2**.

Figure 2

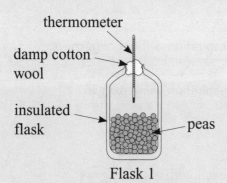

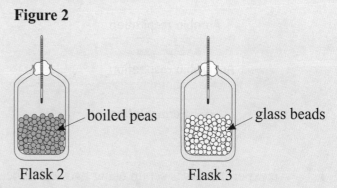

Flask 1   Flask 2   Flask 3

The student records the temperature of each flask at the beginning of the experiment (day 0), then every day for three days.

Table 1 shows her results.

Table 1

Day	Temperature (°C)		
	Flask 1	Flask 2	Flask 3
Day 0	20	20	20
Day 1	23	20	20
Day 2	25	21	20
Day 3	28	22	20

3.1 Give **two** variables that the student needed to control to make the experiment a fair test.

....

....
                                                                                                   [2]

3.2 The student's results could have been affected by random error.
     Suggest **one** way that the student could reduce the effect of any random error on her results.

....

....
                                                                                                   [1]

3.3 Flasks 2 and 3 are control experiments. Explain why the student included both of these controls.

....

....

....
                                                                                                   [2]

3.4 The student hypothesises that the temperature of flask 2 increased slightly over the course
     of the experiment due to the presence of respiring microorganisms on the surface of the peas.
     Suggest how the student could modify her method in order to test this hypothesis.

....

....
                                                                                                   [1]

                                                                                    [Total 6 marks]

Topic 4 — Bioenergetics

Aerobic and Anaerobic Respiration

Draw lines to match up each process on the left with its correct description on the right.

Aerobic respiration

Anaerobic respiration

Fermentation

Respiration without oxygen.

Respiration using oxygen.

1 An experiment was set up using two sealed beakers, each with a carbon dioxide monitor attached. The set up is shown in **Figure 1**.

Figure 1

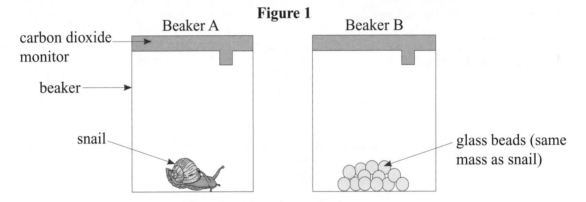

Beaker A   Beaker B

carbon dioxide monitor

beaker

snail

glass beads (same mass as snail)

The percentage (%) of carbon dioxide in the air in both beakers was measured at the start of the experiment and again after 2 hours. The results are shown in **Table 1**.

Table 1

Time (hours)	% carbon dioxide in the air	
	Beaker A	Beaker B
0	0.04	0.04
2	0.10	0.04

1.1 Suggest **one** ethical consideration that must be taken into account during this experiment.

....

[1]

1.2 Describe and explain the results for Beaker A.

....

....

[1]

1.3 Describe and explain the results for Beaker B.

....

....

[1]

1.4 What would have happened to the level of oxygen in Beaker A after two hours?
Explain your answer.

....

....

[2]

1.5 In the experiment, Beaker B was set up in the same way as Beaker A but with
glass beads instead of a snail. Suggest why Beaker B is used in the experiment.

....

....

[1]

[Total 6 marks]

2 *S. cerevisiae* is a type of yeast. It carries out fermentation. **Grade 6-7**

2.1 Complete the following word equation for fermentation.

.... → ethanol + carbon dioxide

[1]

2.2 For each of the products of fermentation in yeast, outline **one** industrial use.

Product ....

Industrial use ....

Product ....

Industrial use ....

[2]

[Total 3 marks]

3 **Figure 2** shows a muscle cell. **Grade 6-7**
Compare aerobic respiration and anaerobic respiration in muscle cells.

Figure 2

....

....

....

....

....

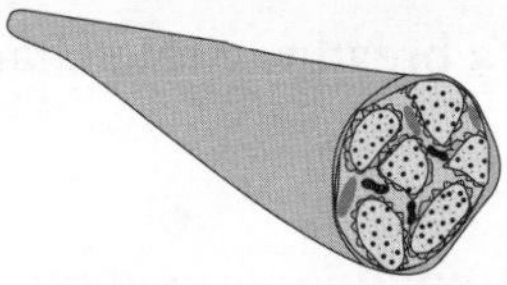

[Total 3 marks]

Exam Tip

To get the marks for 'compare' questions, you need to make sure each point you make mentions both the things you're comparing. For example, if you were asked to compare your brother and sister*, 'my brother is tall' wouldn't get any marks, but 'my brother is taller than my sister' might well just get a mark. (*Unlikely to be a real exam question, sorry.)

Topic 4 — Bioenergetics

Exercise

Choose from the words on the right to complete the
sentences about exercise. Some words may not be used at all.

carbon dioxide   oxygen

aerobically   lactic acid   urea

oxygen debt   muscles

During exercise your .... may respire anaerobically resulting in an

.... This is the amount of extra .... your body

needs to react with the build up of .... and remove it from cells.

1   A student was investigating the effect of exercise on his own breathing rate.
    He counted his number of breaths per minute before, during and after a period of exercise.
    He repeated his experiment another two times. The results are shown in **Table 1** below.

Table 1

	Breathing rate (number of breaths per minute)			
	Before exercise	During exercise	One minute after exercise	Five minutes after exercise
	11	16	15	12
	12	15	14	11
	11	15	14	12
Mean	11	15	14	

1.1 Calculate the mean breathing rate five minutes after exercise.

Mean = ... breaths per minute

[1]

1.2 Describe and explain how the student's breathing rate changed during exercise compared to
     before exercise, as shown in **Table 1**.

     ....

     ....

     ....

[3]

1.3 Describe and explain how the student's breathing rate changed after exercise compared to
     during exercise, as shown in **Table 1**.

     ....

     ....

     ....

     ....

[5]

1.4 Give **two** other variables that the student could have measured which would have shown the same trend as breathing rate during exercise.

....

[2]

[Total 11 marks]

2 **Figure 1** below shows the amount of lactic acid in an athlete's body before, during and after some vigorous exercise.

Grade
7-9

Figure 1

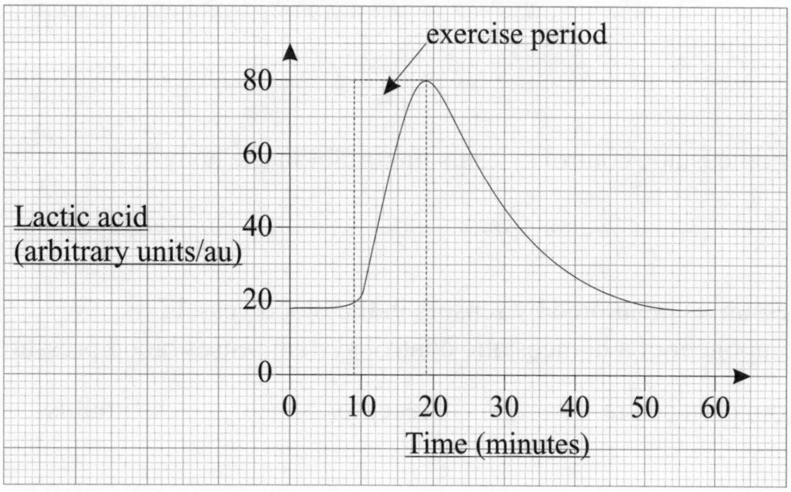

2.1 The amount of lactic acid increases from 20 au to 80 au across the duration of the exercise period. Work out the percentage change in lactic acid during this time.

Percentage change = ...%

[2]

2.2 Explain why there was an increase in lactic acid during the exercise period.

....

....

....

[3]

2.3 What physical effects does a long period of vigorous exercise have on muscles?

....

....

[2]

2.4 The amount of lactic acid in the athlete's body decreases between 20 and 60 minutes. Explain how this lactic acid is cleared from the body.

....

....

[2]

[Total 9 marks]

Exam Tip

It's easy to make small mistakes in calculations when you're in that exam hall, so it's really important to show all your working. That way, even if you do make a mistake, at least you might still get some marks for how you worked it out.

Homeostasis

1 Human blood pressure is maintained by a homeostatic control system. *Grade 6-7*

1.1 What is homeostasis?

....

....

....
[2]

1.2 Why are homeostatic control systems important in the body?

....
[1]

1.3 Blood pressure is monitored by sensors in the blood vessels.
Which component of a homeostatic control system senses blood pressure? Tick **one** box.

☐ coordination centre ☐ receptor ☐ stimulus ☐ effector
[1]

1.4 Outline the stages in the negative feedback mechanism when blood pressure becomes too high.

....

....

....
[3]

[Total 7 marks]

2 A person's skin temperature was measured over a 50 minute period. *Grade 6-7*

During that time, the person began exercising. They then returned to a resting state before the end of the investigation. **Figure 1** shows the change in the person's skin temperature over the 50 minutes.

Figure 1

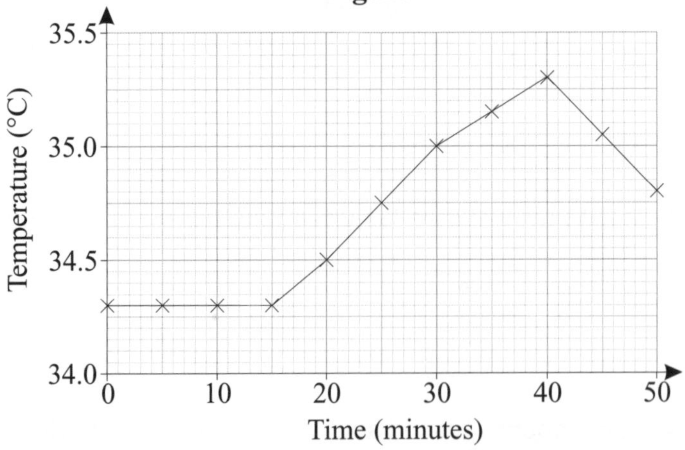

Temperature (°C) vs Time (minutes)

2.1 Suggest the time at which the person began exercising.

....
[1]

2.2 Calculate the rate at which the temperature increased between 20 and 30 minutes.

Rate = ...°C/min
[2]

[Total 3 marks]

The Nervous System

1 **Figure 1** shows part of the human nervous system. (Grade 4-6)

1.1 Name the structures labelled **X** and **Y** on **Figure 1**.

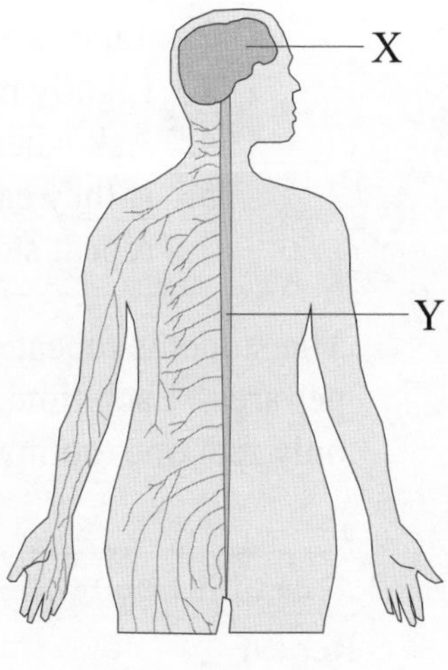

X ....

Y ....

[2]

1.2 Which part of the nervous system do structures **X** and **Y** form?

....

[1]

1.3 What is the role of the part of the nervous system formed by structures **X** and **Y**?

....

....

[1]

[Total 4 marks]

Figure 1

2 Multicellular organisms such as humans have a nervous system. (Grade 6-7)

2.1 What is the function of the nervous system in humans?

....

....

[2]

2.2 Receptor cells in the eye are sensitive to light.
For a nervous system response in the eye, state whether each of the following features is a stimulus, a coordinator or a response.

Spinal cord ....

Bright light ....

Blinking ....

[3]

2.3 Name the **two** main types of neurones found in humans outside the central nervous system.

....

....

[2]

2.4 Name **two** types of effector and state how they respond to nervous impulses.

....

....

[2]

[Total 9 marks]

Target AO3

3   Two students are investigating the sensitivity of the skin on different areas of the body using the method below.

> 1. Blindfold the person to be tested.
> 2. Tape two toothpicks onto a ruler so that they are 50 mm apart.
> 3. Lightly press the two toothpicks onto the person's arm.
> 4. Ask whether the person can feel one or two toothpicks.
> 5. If they can feel two toothpicks, move the toothpicks 5 mm closer together and repeat steps 3 and 4. Keep doing this until they can only feel one toothpick.

The students repeated the experiment for different areas of the body, and repeated it three times per area. Each time, they recorded the distance between the toothpicks at which the person could only feel one toothpick. Their results are shown in **Table 1**.

Table 1

Area of the body	Forearm			Palm			Back of hand		
Repeat	1	2	3	1	2	3	1	2	3
Distance between toothpicks (mm)	30	30	45	5	5	5	25	20	15

3.1 The students calculated the mean distance between toothpicks for each area of the body. Explain why the students repeated their readings and calculated a mean for each area.

....

....

[1]

3.2 Calculate the uncertainty in the students' results for the back of the hand.

.... mm

[2]

3.3 Suggest how the accuracy of this experiment could be improved.

....

....

[1]

3.4 The students think that the third repeat reading for the forearm is an anomalous result. Suggest how the students could confirm that the result is anomalous.

....

....

[1]

3.5 The students conclude from their results that the palm is the most sensitive part of the body. Explain why this is **not** a valid conclusion.

....

....

[2]

[Total 7 marks]

Topic 5 — Homeostasis and Response

Synapses and Reflexes

Warm-Up

Circle the examples that are reflex reactions.

Pedalling a bike.   The pupil widening in dim light.

Dropping a hot plate.   Running to catch a bus.   Writing a letter.

1   Which of the following sentences is correct? Tick **one** box.   (Grade 4-6)

☐ Reflex reactions are slow and under conscious control.

☐ Reflex reactions are slow and automatic.

☐ Reflex reactions are rapid and automatic.

☐ Reflex reactions are rapid and under conscious control.

[Total 1 mark]

2   **Figure 1** shows a reflex arc.   (Grade 4-6)

2.1   Name structures **X**, **Y** and **Z**.

X ....

Y ....

Z ....

[3]

Figure 1

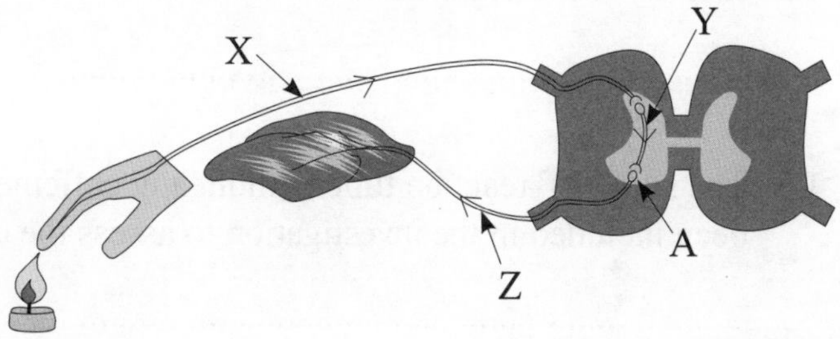

2.2   In the reflex arc shown in **Figure 1**, name:

the stimulus ....

the coordinator ....

the effector ....

[3]

2.3   Structure **A** is the junction between two neurones. Name structure **A**.

....

[1]

2.4   How is a nerve signal transmitted across this junction?

....

[1]

[Total 8 marks]

Exam Tip

If an exam question asks you to 'name' something like a structure or process, don't start writing an essay. In fact, you can stay clear of explaining or describing anything at all. A little word or phrase is all the examiners are looking for.

Topic 5 — Homeostasis and Response

Investigating Reaction Time

1 Stimulants, such as caffeine, increase the rate at which nerve impulses travel. An investigation was carried out to assess the impact of different caffeinated drinks on reaction time.

The investigation involved measuring reaction time using a ruler drop test. In this test, a ruler is held above a student's outstretched hand by another person. The ruler is then dropped without warning and the student catches the ruler as quickly as possible. The distance down the ruler where the student caught it is used to calculate their reaction time in seconds (s).

Three different students (Students **1** to **3**) consumed a different caffeinated drink — each one contained a different amount of caffeine. Each student then undertook three ruler drop tests. The results are shown in the table below.

1.1 Calculate the mean reaction time for Student **2** and Student **3**.

Student **2** = ... s

Student **3** = ... s

[2]

	Reaction time (s)		
	Student 1	Student 2	Student 3
Test 1	0.09	0.16	0.20
Test 2	0.10	0.13	0.22
Test 3	0.43	0.15	0.19
Mean	0.21		

1.2 Identify the anomalous result in the table.

....

[1]

1.3 The students' reaction time without any caffeine was **not** measured. Explain why it should have been included in the investigation to assess the effect of each caffeinated drink.

....

....

....

[2]

1.4 Explain why the results of this investigation can't be used to **compare** the effect of the three different caffeinated drinks on reaction time.

....

....

[2]

1.5 An alternative version of the investigation was carried out. This time, the effect of a set quantity of caffeine on the reaction times of different individuals was investigated. Reaction times of three different students were measured, both before and after the consumption of caffeine.
Give **three** variables that should have been controlled in this investigation.

....

....

....

[3]

[Total 10 marks]

Topic 5 — Homeostasis and Response

The Brain

1   The brain has different regions that carry out different functions.   (Grade 4-6)

1.1   Name the type of cell that makes up most of the brain's material.

....

[1]

1.2   Name the region of the brain that controls unconscious activities.

....

[1]

1.3   State **two** activities that take place in the human body which are not under our conscious control.

....

....

[2]

[Total 4 marks]

2   **Figure 1** shows the human brain. Labels **A**, **B** and **C** point to three different regions.   (Grade 6-7)

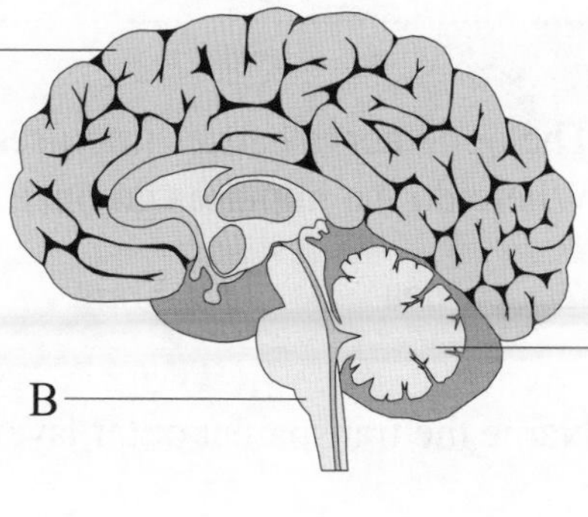

2.1   A hospital patient has had damage to her brain. She is having problems understanding words. Which region of the brain is damaged? Tick **one** box.

☐ A   ☐ B   ☐ C

[1]

Figure 1

A—   C   B—

2.2   Which region of the brain controls the heartbeat? Tick **one** box.

☐ A   ☐ B   ☐ C

[1]

2.3   Suggest **two** reasons why it is difficult to investigate and treat brain disorders.

....

....

[2]

Scientists have been able to map regions of the brain to their functions using MRI scanning.

2.4   State **two** other ways scientists can gather information to map the regions of the brain to particular functions.

....

....

[2]

[Total 6 marks]

The Eye

Warm-Up

Use the words below to correctly label the diagram of the eye.
You don't have to use every word, but each word can only be used once.

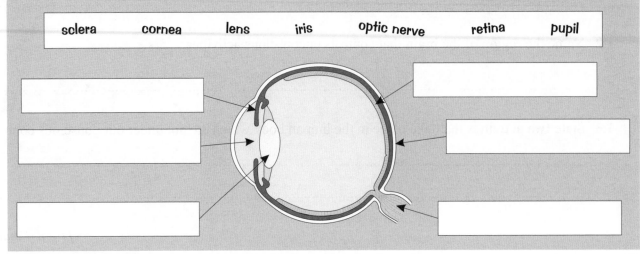

sclera   cornea   lens   iris   optic nerve   retina   pupil

1   The eye is a sense organ containing receptors. Grade 4-6

1.1   Which part of the eye contains receptor cells that are sensitive to light?

    ....

    [1]

1.2   The optic nerve carries impulses.
    Where do the impulses go once they have left the retina? Tick **one** box.

    ☐ cornea   ☐ brain   ☐ sclera   ☐ lens

    [1]

1.3   Name the transparent outer layer at the front of the eye.

    ....

    [1]

1.4   Which part of the eye controls the size of the pupil?

    ....

    [1]

1.5   Which **two** parts of the eye change the shape of the lens during focussing?

    ....

    ....

    [2]

    [Total 6 marks]

Exam Tip

If a multiple choice question tells you to 'tick one box' then you know that only one of the options is right. If you don't know the answer, it might be helpful to cross out any options that you know are definitely <u>not</u> right so you have fewer to think about. And if you're really stumped, don't leave the tick boxes blank — you might as well have your best guess.

Topic 5 — Homeostasis and Response

2   **Figure 1** shows a human eye as it would appear in two different light levels.

Figure 1

A      B

2.1 How does the appearance of eye A in **Figure 1** differ from eye B?

....

....

                                                                          [2]

2.2 Which eye, A or B, is in a lower light level? Explain your answer.

....

....

                                                                          [1]

2.3 Explain why it is important for the changes between A and B to take place.

....

....

                                                                          [2]

                                                              [Total 5 marks]

3*   Describe how the process of accommodation in the human eye works to:
•   focus on a near object,
•   focus on a distant object.   Grade 7-9
Include details of the structures of the eye involved and their functions.

....

....

....

....

....

....

....

....

....

....

                                                              [Total 6 marks]

Exam Tip

Long-answer questions can feel a bit daunting, particularly if they're worth six marks. But don't panic — just read
the question carefully and underline any key bits that you need to cover. There might be some bullet points telling
you exactly what the examiners want. If there are, make sure you make the most of it and cover everything there.

Correcting Vision Defects

1   Some people have to wear spectacle lenses to correct a defect in their vision.
Figure 1 shows how spectacle lenses can be used to correct vision defects.

Figure 1

A   **B**

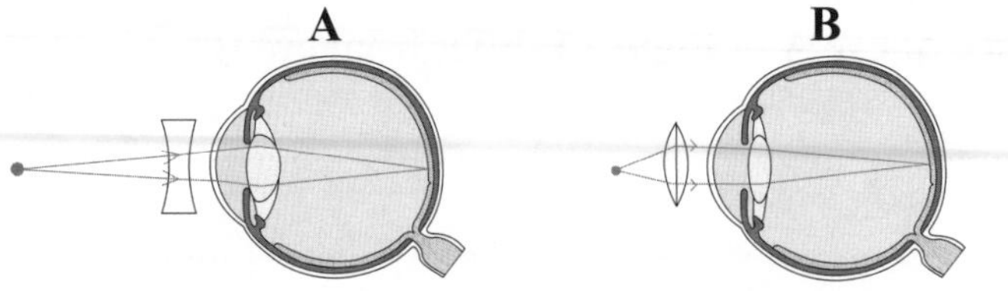

1.1   What vision defect is person **A** in **Figure 1** suffering from?

....

[1]

1.2   Explain how a spectacle lens corrects the sight of a person with this vision defect.

....

....

[2]

1.3   Describe where the rays of light focus in the uncorrected eye of person B in **Figure 1**.

....

[1]

1.4   Name the shape of the spectacle lens used to correct the vision defect of person B.

....

[1]

[Total 5 marks]

2   New technologies are now available to correct vision defects.

2.1   Explain how laser technology can be used to correct vision defects.

....

....

[2]

2.2   State **one** other new technology that offers a permanent correction for vision defects.

....

[1]

2.3   Suggest **one** risk of the procedure named in part 2.2.

....

[1]

2.4   A person is suffering from long-sightedness but does not want to wear spectacles or
undergo a permanent procedure. What might an optician recommend for this person?

....

[1]

[Total 5 marks]

Controlling Body Temperature

1 The body's thermoregulatory centre monitors and controls body temperature. *Grade 4-6*

1.1 Name the organ of the body where the thermoregulatory centre is located.

....

[1]

1.2 The thermoregulatory centre contains receptors.
What are these receptors used to monitor?

....

[1]

1.3 Briefly outline how the thermoregulatory centre receives information about the temperature outside the body.

....

....

[2]

[Total 4 marks]

2 The body has several responses to regulate body temperature. *Grade 6-7*

2.1 Explain how these responses bring about a change in body temperature if the temperature becomes too high.

....

....

....

....

[3]

2.2 Explain how these responses bring about a change in body temperature if the temperature becomes too low.

....

....

....

....

[3]

[Total 6 marks]

Exam Tip

In the exam, you might be asked to explain how the body's temperature regulation mechanisms would respond in a certain situation, e.g. during a cycle race. For these questions, think about what's happening to the body's temperature — if it's going up (e.g. because increased respiration is warming the body), the body's going to want to cool down, and vice versa.

Topic 5 — Homeostasis and Response

74

3 A scientist is using a model to investigate how sweating cools the body.

The scientist fills two boiling tubes with hot water. She wraps one boiling tube with a wet paper towel and the other with a dry paper towel. She records the temperature of the water in each boiling tube every minute. The results of the experiment are shown in **Table 1**.

Table 1

Time (min)	Dry (°C)	Wet (°C)
0	60	60
1	58	54
2	56	49
3	55	45
4	53	38
5	52	39
6	50	36
7	49	34
8	47	32
9	46	30
10	45	29

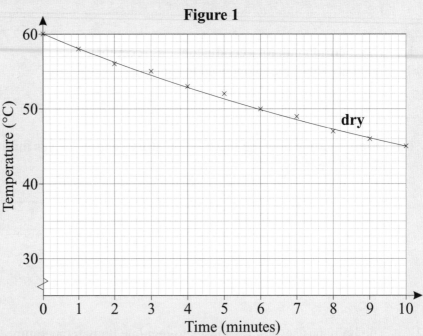

Figure 1

3.1 Plot the results for the boiling tube with the wet paper towel on **Figure 1**. Include a curved line of best fit.

[3]

3.2 Describe what the results of the experiment show.

....

....

[1]

3.3 Give **two** variables that the scientist should have controlled during the experiment.

....

....

[2]

3.4 Suggest how the scientist's experiment acts as a model for sweating.

....

....

....

[3]

[Total 9 marks]

Exam Tip

Plotting a graph can get you easy marks in an exam. Just make sure you double-check the scales on the axes before you start plotting the points — and draw those points neatly, using a sharp pencil. If you have to draw a curve of best fit, it should be one smooth, continuous line. Draw it in pencil too, so that you have the chance to redo it if it goes wrong.

The Endocrine System

1 The endocrine system is a collection of glands in the body that secrete hormones. **Grade 4-6**

1.1 Which of the following statements about glands is correct? Tick **one** box.

☐ Glands secrete hormones directly into cells.

☐ Glands secrete hormones directly into tissues.

☐ Glands secrete hormones directly into the blood.

☐ Glands secrete hormones directly into organs.

[1]

1.2 Which of the following statements best describes hormones?
Tick **one** box.

☐ Hormones are tissues. ☐ Hormones are chemical molecules.

☐ Hormones are cells. ☐ Hormones are enzymes.

[1]

1.3 State **two** ways in which the effects of the endocrine system differ from the nervous system.

....

....

[2]

[Total 4 marks]

2 **Figure 1** shows the positions of some glands in the human body. **Grade 4-6**

2.1 Name glands A to E in **Figure 1**.

A ....

B ....

C ....

D ....

E ....

[5]

Figure 1

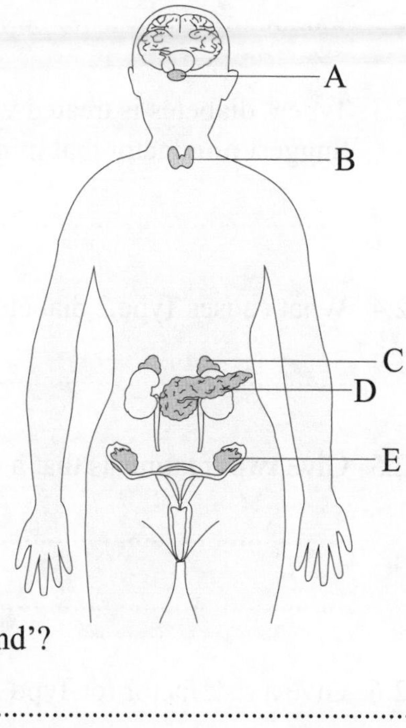

The 'master gland' secretes several hormones
into the blood in response to body conditions.

2.2 What is the name of the 'master gland'?

....

[1]

2.3 What is the function of the hormones released by the 'master gland'?

....

....

[2]

[Total 8 marks]

Controlling Blood Glucose

1 The concentration of glucose in the blood is controlled by hormones. *(Grade 4-6)*

1.1 Which gland in the human body monitors and controls blood glucose concentration?
Tick **one** box.

☐ pancreas ☐ pituitary gland ☐ thyroid ☐ testis

[1]

1.2 Which hormone is produced when blood glucose concentration becomes too high?

....

[1]

1.3 Describe what happens to excess glucose in the blood.

....

....

[2]

[Total 4 marks]

2 Diabetes exists in two different forms, Type 1 and Type 2. *(Grade 6-7)*

2.1 What causes Type 1 diabetes?

....

[1]

2.2 What is the defining characteristic of Type 1 diabetes?

....

[1]

2.3 Type 1 diabetes is treated with insulin injections.
Suggest **one** factor that might affect the amount of insulin injected by a patient.

....

[1]

2.4 What causes Type 2 diabetes?

....

[1]

2.5 Give **two** treatments that a doctor would recommend for Type 2 diabetes.

....

....

[2]

2.6 Give a risk factor for Type 2 diabetes.

....

[1]

[Total 7 marks]

3   In an experiment, the blood glucose concentration of a person without diabetes was recorded at regular intervals in a 90 minute time period. Fifteen minutes into the experiment, a glucose drink was given. **Figure 1** shows the results of the experiment.

Figure 1

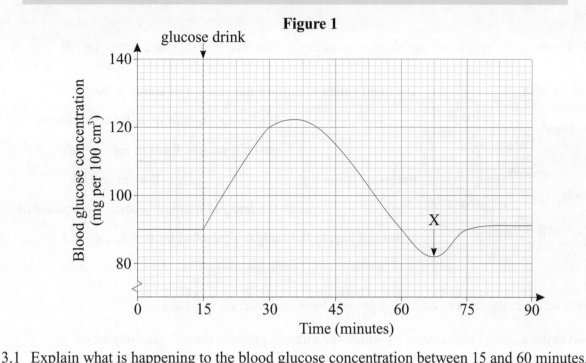

3.1   Explain what is happening to the blood glucose concentration between 15 and 60 minutes.

....

....

....

[3]

3.2   Name the hormone being released by the pancreas at point **X** on the graph.

....

[1]

3.3   Describe the effect that hormone **X** has on the blood glucose concentration.

....

[1]

3.4   Explain how hormone **X** causes this effect.

....

....

[1]

3.5   Suggest how the shape of the graph would differ if the person had Type 1 diabetes.

....

....

[1]

[Total 7 marks]

Topic 5 — Homeostasis and Response

The Kidneys

Fill in the gaps in this passage about controlling water content. Use words from the left.

pancreas

kidneys

blood

enzymes

osmosis

cells

ions

active transport

The body needs to control the amount of water in the

.... The wrong amount of water can damage

.... because it causes them to lose or gain

too much water by .... The amount of

.... in the body also affects cells. The amount of

water and ions in the body is controlled by the ....

1   Unwanted substances are removed from the body in the urine.   (Grade 4-6)

1.1   What is the name of the process by which the kidneys produce urine? Tick **one** box.

☐   active transport

☐   filtration

☐   osmosis

☐   diffusion

[1]

1.2   The unwanted substances removed in the urine include excess water and some ions.
Which other substance is also removed via the kidneys in the urine?

....

[1]

A process in the kidneys returns useful substances to the blood so that they are not lost in urine.

1.3   What is the name of this process?

....

[1]

1.4   Name **two** useful substances that are returned to the blood by this process.

....

....

[2]

[Total 5 marks]

2   Some water leaves the body in the urine. Water can also be lost from the skin by sweating.   (Grade 4-6)

2.1   Give **one** other way that water can be lost from the body.

....

[1]

Topic 5 — Homeostasis and Response

2.2 Name **two** substances other than water that are lost through the skin in sweat.

....

[2]

2.3 Which of the following statements is true? Tick **one** box.

☐ The body can control water loss from the skin.

☐ The body can only control water loss from the skin at night.

☐ The body can't control water loss from the skin.

[1]

[Total 4 marks]

3 Excess amino acids in the body are broken down. Grade 4-6

3.1 In which organ of the body are the excess amino acids broken down?

....

[1]

3.2 What is the source of these excess amino acids?

....

[1]

3.3 Deamination forms part of the breakdown process. Name the waste product of deamination.

....

[1]

3.4 Explain why this waste product is converted into urea for excretion as soon as it is formed.

....

[1]

[Total 4 marks]

4* The body is constantly monitoring and regulating its water content. Describe the body's response when the brain detects that the water content is too low. Include details of any hormones and structures involved. Grade 7-9

....

....

....

....

....

....

....

[Total 4 marks]

Exam Tip

If you realise you've missed something out of a long answer, be careful about squashing it in — remember, if the examiners can't read what you've written, they can't award you marks. A neat way to add in an extra bit is to put an asterisk (*) where the missing point needs to go, and then put another asterisk underneath your answer with what you want to say.

Topic 5 — Homeostasis and Response

Kidney Failure

1 **Figure 1** shows the operation of a dialysis machine.

Figure 1

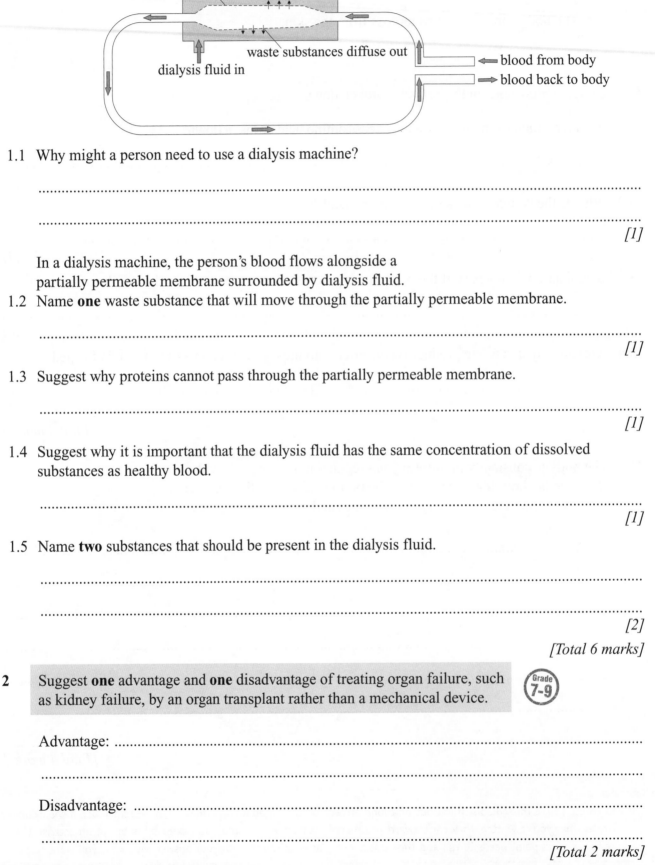

partially permeable membrane   dialysis fluid out

waste substances diffuse out

dialysis fluid in

blood from body

blood back to body

1.1 Why might a person need to use a dialysis machine?

....

....

[1]

In a dialysis machine, the person's blood flows alongside a
partially permeable membrane surrounded by dialysis fluid.

1.2 Name **one** waste substance that will move through the partially permeable membrane.

....

[1]

1.3 Suggest why proteins cannot pass through the partially permeable membrane.

....

[1]

1.4 Suggest why it is important that the dialysis fluid has the same concentration of dissolved
substances as healthy blood.

....

[1]

1.5 Name **two** substances that should be present in the dialysis fluid.

....

....

[2]

[Total 6 marks]

2 Suggest **one** advantage and **one** disadvantage of treating organ failure, such
as kidney failure, by an organ transplant rather than a mechanical device.

Advantage: ....

....

Disadvantage: ....

....

[Total 2 marks]

Puberty and the Menstrual Cycle

1   The release of sex hormones begins at puberty.   (Grade 4-6)

1.1   What is the name of the main female hormone produced in the ovary? Tick **one** box.

☐ progesterone   ☐ oestrogen   ☐ luteinising hormone   ☐ follicle stimulating hormone

[1]

1.2   What is the name of the process by which eggs are released from the ovary?

....

[1]

1.3   How often is an egg released from an ovary? Tick **one** box.

☐ Every 7 days.   ☐ Every 14 days.   ☐ Every 21 days.   ☐ Every 28 days.

[1]

1.4   Name the hormone that stimulates the release of an egg.

....

[1]

1.5   Name the hormone that stimulates sperm production in men.

....

[1]

1.6   Where in the male body is this hormone produced?

....

[1]

[Total 6 marks]

2   Four main hormones interact with each other in the control of the menstrual cycle.   (Grade 6-7)

2.1   Which two hormones are involved in maintaining the uterus lining?

....

....

[2]

2.2   What is the name of the gland that secretes follicle stimulating hormone (FSH)?

....

[1]

2.3   State **two** effects of FSH during the menstrual cycle of a woman.

....

....

[2]

2.4   Which hormone stimulates the release of luteinising hormone (LH)?

....

[1]

[Total 6 marks]

😕 ☐   🙂 ☐   😊 ☐

Topic 5 — Homeostasis and Response

Controlling Fertility

Sort the methods of contraception into the correct places in the table.

abstinence

contraceptive injection

condom

diaphragm

plastic intrauterine device

sterilisation

contraceptive patch

Hormonal	Non-hormonal

1 Some methods of contraception use hormones to control the fertility of a woman. **(Grade 4-6)**

1.1 How is an oral contraceptive taken into the body? Tick **one** box.

☐ As an injection.

☐ As a tablet taken by mouth.

☐ Through the skin from a patch.

[1]

1.2 How do oral contraceptives containing multiple hormones prevent pregnancy? Tick **one** box.

☐ The hormones inhibit oestrogen production.

☐ The hormones inhibit FSH production.

☐ The hormones inhibit LH production.

[1]

1.3 The contraceptive implant is inserted under the skin of the arm.
Which hormone does it release?

....

[1]

1.4 How does the hormone released by the contraceptive implant prevent pregnancy?

....

[1]

[Total 4 marks]

Remember to read all the different options in multiple choice questions. Don't be tempted to dive right in and tick the first option that you think sounds right — sometimes there'll only be slight differences in the wording of different options.

2 Fertility can be controlled by non-hormonal methods of contraception. **Grade 4-6**

2.1 Name a barrier method of contraception that can be used by men.

....

[1]

2.2 Name a barrier method of contraception that can be used by women.

....

[1]

2.3 How do barrier methods of contraception prevent a woman becoming pregnant?

....

[1]

2.4 What is the name given to chemicals that kill or disable sperm?

....

[1]

2.5 A couple not wishing to have children do not want to use any form of contraception.
Suggest how they could avoid pregnancy.

....

[1]

2.6 Name a surgical method of controlling fertility that can be carried out in both men and women.

....

[1]

2.7 Name a barrier method of contraception that protects against sexually transmitted infections.

....

[1]

[Total 7 marks]

3 A woman is considering which contraceptive to use. **Grade 7-9**

3.1 Suggest **one** advantage of choosing the contraceptive injection over the contraceptive pill.

....

[1]

3.2 Suggest **one** disadvantage of choosing the contraceptive injection over the contraceptive pill.

....

[1]

3.3 Suggest **one** advantage of choosing a barrier method of contraception over a hormonal
contraceptive.

....

[1]

[Total 3 marks]

Topic 5 — Homeostasis and Response

More on Controlling Fertility

1 A couple want to have children but the woman has not yet become
pregnant. Blood tests have shown that she has a low level of
follicle stimulating hormone (FSH). She is treated with a fertility drug.

1.1 Explain why a low level of FSH may be preventing the woman from becoming pregnant.

....

.... *[1]*

1.2 In addition to FSH, which other hormone will the fertility drug contain
to help the woman become pregnant? Give a reason for your answer.

....

....

.... *[2]*

1.3 Suggest **one** advantage and **one** disadvantage of this method of fertility treatment.

Advantage: ....

Disadvantage: ....

[2]

[Total 5 marks]

2 *In vitro* fertilisation is a reproductive treatment that
can help people with fertility problems have children.

2.1 Describe the stages involved in a course of *in vitro* fertilisation treatment.

....

....

....

....

....

....

....

....

[5]

2.2 Give **two** disadvantages of *in vitro* fertilisation treatment.

....

....

....

[2]

[Total 7 marks]

Topic 5 — Homeostasis and Response

Adrenaline and Thyroxine

Warm-Up

The graph below shows the change in the level of a hormone
controlled by a negative feedback response over time.
Use the words on the right to fill in the labels on the graph.

normal   low   stimulated

inhibited   high

....
level of hormone
detected

release of hormone ....

Blood hormone level

.... level
of hormone

.... level
of hormone detected

Time

release of hormone ....

1   Thyroxine is a hormone.   *Grade 4-6*

1.1   Which statement best describes the role of thyroxine in the body? Tick **one** box.

☐   Thyroxine inhibits development.

☐   Thyroxine regulates basal metabolic rate.

☐   Thyroxine decreases heart rate.

[1]

1.2   Which gland produces thyroxine?

....

[1]

[Total 2 marks]

2   The hormone adrenaline is produced in times of fear or stress.   *Grade 6-7*

2.1   Where is adrenaline released from?

....

[1]

2.2   Describe the effect that adrenaline has on the body.

....

....

....

[3]

2.3   Name the response that adrenaline prepares the body for.

....

[1]

[Total 5 marks]

Topic 5 — Homeostasis and Response

Plant Hormones

PRACTICAL

1 Two sets of cress seedlings were allowed to germinate under identical environmental conditions.

Grade 6-7

Figure 1

Set A

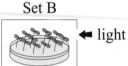

Set B

← light

When the newly germinated shoots were 3 cm tall, the two sets of seedlings were treated as follows:

- The cress seedlings in set A received continuous all-round light.
- The cress seedlings in set B were placed in a box with a slit in one side so that they received light from one side only.

The results are shown in **Figure 1**.

1.1 Compare the growth of the seedlings in Set A with those in Set B.

....

[1]

1.2 What name is given to the response shown by the shoots in Set B?

....

[1]

1.3 Suggest **one** advantage to the plant of this response.

....

[1]

Auxin is a hormone that controls the growth of a plant in response to light.

1.4 Explain the results for Set B. Refer to auxin in your answer.

....

....

....

[3]

[Total 6 marks]

2 A tropism is growth by plants in response to a stimulus. Tropisms are positive when the plant, or part of the plant, grows towards a stimulus. They are negative when the plant, or part of the plant, grows away from a stimulus.

Grade 7-9

2.1 What type of tropism is shown by a root growing towards gravity?

....

[1]

2.2 Name a part of a plant that shows a negative tropism in response to gravity.

....

[1]

2.3 In which direction does a root showing negative phototropism grow?

....

[1]

[Total 3 marks]

Topic 5 — Homeostasis and Response

Target AO3

3 A student is investigating how the tip of a plant shoot affects its growth. Grade 7-9

He sets up four groups of seedlings (Groups A-D), as shown in **Figure 2**.

Figure 2

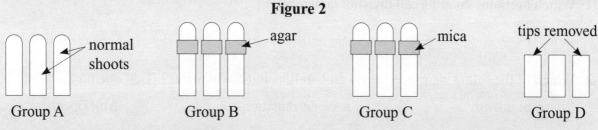

Group A   Group B   Group C   Group D

The tips of the shoots in Group B were cut off and a piece of agar was placed between the tip and the rest of the shoot. The same was done to Group C, but using mica instead of agar. Agar lets water-soluble substances such as auxin pass through it, while mica does not. Group D had the tips of the shoots cut off and nothing was added.

After one week, the shoots in Groups A and B had grown, while the shoots in Groups C and D had not grown.

3.1 Explain the purpose of **Group C** in the experiment.

....

....

[1]

3.2 The student's hypothesis was:
"Removing the tips of the shoots will stop them growing because auxin has been removed."
Do the results of the experiment support the student's hypothesis? Explain your answer.

....

....

....

....

....

[3]

3.3 Suggest a further experiment that the student could do to provide support for his hypothesis.

....

....

....

....

[2]

[Total 6 marks]

Exam Tip

Figuring out what's going on in an experiment you're not familiar with can be pretty tricky. Make sure you read all the information the question gives you carefully — try underlining the key words in the method to help you make sense of it.

Topic 5 — Homeostasis and Response

Commercial Uses of Plant Hormones

1 Plants produce hormones to coordinate and control a variety of processes. **Grade 4-6**

1.1 Which hormone controls cell division in plants?

....

[1]

1.2 Which of the following processes do gibberellins initiate in plants? Tick **one** box.

☐ root growth ☐ seed germination ☐ fruit ripening

[1]

[Total 2 marks]

2 Give **three** uses of gibberellins in horticulture. **Grade 4-6**

....

....

....

[Total 3 marks]

3 The bananas in UK supermarkets often come from countries abroad, such as Ecuador. **Grade 6-7**

3.1 Name the hormone commonly used in the food industry to control the ripening of fruit.

....

[1]

3.2 Suggest why bananas destined for UK supermarkets are picked before they are ripe.

....

....

[2]

[Total 3 marks]

4 A gardener wants to clone a plant in his garden. He takes a cutting of the plant and dips it into a powder containing a particular hormone. **Grade 6-7**

4.1 Suggest which hormone the powder contains.

....

[1]

4.2 Suggest what the powder is for.

....

[1]

4.3 What other product might the gardener use in his garden that may contain this hormone?

....

[1]

[Total 3 marks]

Topic 5 — Homeostasis and Response

DNA

1 DNA makes up the genetic material in animal and plant cells. *Grade 4-6*

1.1 Which of the following statements about DNA is correct? Tick **one** box.

☐ DNA is located in the cytoplasm of animal and plant cells.

☐ DNA is located in the ribosomes in animal and plant cells.

☐ DNA is located in the nucleus of animal and plant cells.

☐ DNA is located in vacuoles in animal and plant cells.

[1]

1.2 What are chromosomes? Tick **one** box.

☐ Proteins coded for by DNA.

☐ The structures that contain DNA.

☐ The site of protein synthesis.

☐ The bases that make up DNA.

[1]

[Total 2 marks]

2 An organism's DNA contains lots of sections called genes. *Grade 6-7*

2.1 Outline the function of genes.

....

....

[2]

2.2 What is meant by the term 'genome'?

....

....

[1]

2.3 Give **one** reason why it is important for scientists to have an understanding of the human genome. Explain your answer.

....

....

....

....

....

[2]

[Total 5 marks]

Exam Tip

To properly understand this topic, you need to know how DNA, genes, genomes, chromosomes, proteins and amino acids all relate to each other. Once you've got that sussed, it'll make answering the questions a whole lot easier.

 ☐   ☐ ☺ ☐

The Structure of DNA and Protein Synthesis

1   DNA is made up of long chains of nucleotides.
Each nucleotide contains one of four DNA bases. *(Grade 6-7)*

1.1   What are the four bases found in DNA?
Tick **one** box.

☐ A, T, P and G   ☐ C, T, G and F   ☐ A, C, G and T   ☐ T, C, A and E

[1]

Figure 1 shows a DNA nucleotide.

Figure 1

1.2   Name the parts labelled A and B.

A: ....

B: ....

[2]

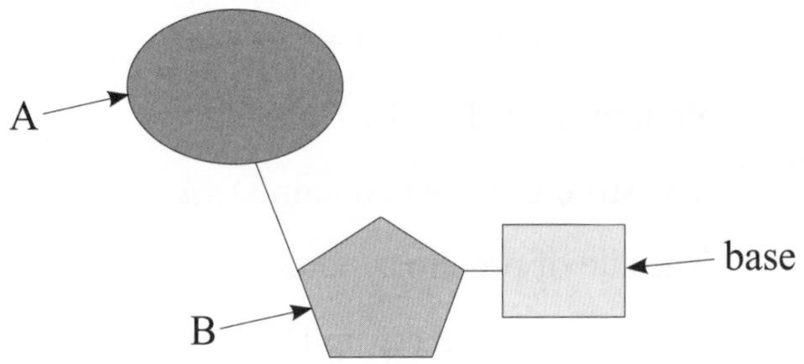

Bases in the two strands that make up a DNA molecule always pair up in the same way.
Figure 2 shows a short piece of DNA.

Figure 2

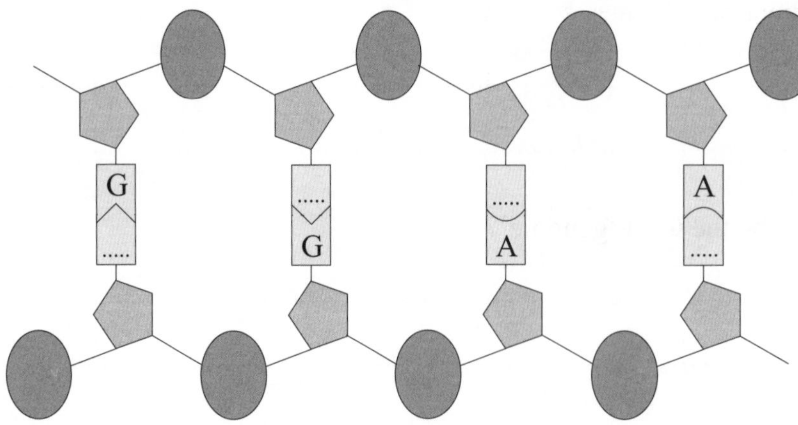

1.3   Complete **Figure 2** by writing the correct letter in the unlabelled bases.

[2]

1.4   Explain how the DNA bases in a gene code for a specific chain of amino acids.

....

....

....

[2]

[Total 7 marks]

Exam Tip

DNA diagrams can be quite hard to interpret — all those shapes and lines... They might not always look <u>exactly</u> like the ones you have in your revision notes, but if you know the three different components of a nucleotide and understand how they link together, you should always be able to decipher what you're being shown.

2 DNA molecules carry the code to make proteins. **(Grade 6-7)**

2.1 Name the structures in a cell where protein synthesis takes place.

....
[1]

2.2 Not all parts of DNA code for amino acids. Some of the DNA is non-coding.
Briefly describe **one** role that non-coding DNA plays in protein synthesis.

....
[1]

[Total 2 marks]

3 DNA is located in the nucleus of the cell. Protein synthesis
takes place outside of the nucleus in the cytoplasm.
DNA molecules are too large to leave the nucleus. **(Grade 6-7)**

3.1 Explain how DNA can be used in the synthesis of proteins when it is unable to leave the nucleus.

....

....

....
[2]

3.2 Describe the process that takes place at the site of protein synthesis to produce
chains of amino acids.

....

....

....
[3]

3.3 Explain what happens to a chain of amino acids once it has been assembled.

....

....
[2]

3.4 Proteins have many jobs. For example, collagen is used to form structures in the body.
Briefly outline the role of **two** other types of protein found in the human body.

....

....

....

....
[4]

[Total 11 marks]

Topic 6 — Inheritance, Variation and Evolution

Mutations

1   Mutations are random changes in the DNA of an organism.

     Figure 1 shows the normal order of bases in a section of DNA and then the same section of DNA after a mutation has occurred.

Figure 1

DNA before mutation: A A G C T T C C A

DNA after mutation: A A G C T T C C G A

1.1   Circle where the mutation has taken place in **Figure 1**.

[1]

1.2   Explain how mutations could lead to a change in the protein being synthesised.

....

....

....

....

[3]

     Mutations can affect the functioning of a protein.

1.3   Suggest **one** possible effect of a mutation that changes the shape of a structural protein.

....

....

[2]

1.4   Suggest **one** possible effect of a mutation in a gene that codes for a particular enzyme.

....

....

....

[3]

[Total 9 marks]

Exam Tip

Sometimes you might get an unusual question — e.g. you might have to circle something, fill in a box or add something to a diagram. Read the question really carefully and make sure you do exactly what it asks — no more and no less.

Topic 6 — Inheritance, Variation and Evolution

Reproduction

1   Reproduction can be sexual or asexual.   (Grade 4-6)

In sexual reproduction, gametes from a male and female fuse together.

1.1   Name the male gamete in animals.

....

[1]

1.2   Name the female gamete in plants.

....

[1]

1.3   Which type of cell division is involved in the production of gametes?

....

[1]

Asexual reproduction does not involve gametes.

1.4   What name can be given to the cells resulting from asexual reproduction?

☐ gametes   ☐ clones   ☐ eggs   ☐ chromosomes

[1]

1.5   Name the type of cell division used in asexual reproduction.

....

[1]

[Total 5 marks]

2   Sexual reproduction involves the fusion of gametes to form a fertilised egg cell.   (Grade 6-7)

2.1   Explain how a fertilised egg cell has the correct number of chromosomes.

....

....

....

[2]

2.2   Asexual and sexual reproduction are very different methods.
Give **four** ways in which asexual reproduction is different to sexual reproduction.

....

....

....

....

....

....

[4]

[Total 6 marks]

 ☐   ☐   ☐   Topic 6 — Inheritance, Variation and Evolution

Meiosis

1 Sexual reproduction in humans involves meiosis. (Grade 4-6)

1.1 Where in the body does meiosis take place?

....

[1]

1.2 What happens to the DNA at the very start of meiosis, before the cell starts to divide?

....

[1]

1.3 How many cell divisions are there during the process of meiosis?

....

[1]

1.4 Briefly describe the results of meiosis.

....

....

....

....

[3]

[Total 6 marks]

2 During fertilisation, two gametes formed by meiosis join together. (Grade 4-6)

2.1 How many copies of each chromosome does the resulting cell have?

....

[1]

After the two gametes join to produce a fertilised egg, the cells divide repeatedly.

2.2 What type of cell division do these cells undergo?

....

[1]

2.3 The dividing cells form an embryo.
What happens to the cells in the embryo as it develops in order to form the whole organism?

....

....

[1]

[Total 3 marks]

Exam Tip

It's outrageously easy to get mixed up between meiosis and mitosis when the pressure is on in an exam. Remember, meiosis is the one that makes — eggs and sperm. Mitosis makes twin (identical) cells. Even if you know the difference, it's still really easy to accidentally write one when you mean the other 'cos the words are so similar, so always check twice.

Topic 6 — Inheritance, Variation and Evolution

More on Reproduction

Complete the passage using words from below. You don't need to use every word.

runners   different   spores   stalks   identical   seeds

Some organisms can reproduce both sexually and asexually. For example, strawberry plants reproduce asexually using .... and reproduce sexually by producing ....

Asexual reproduction in strawberry plants results in genetically .... offspring whereas

sexual reproduction produces genetically .... offspring.

1 Some organisms can reproduce both sexually and asexually. **(Grade 4-6)**

1.1 Daffodils can reproduce by producing seeds or bulbs. Bulbs divide to form new plants.
What type of reproduction is shown when the bulbs divide to produce new plants?

....

[1]

1.2 Which of these statements about the reproduction of the malaria parasite is true?
Tick **one** box.

☐ Malaria parasites reproduce sexually in the human host, but asexually in the mosquito.

☐ Malaria parasites reproduce sexually in both the human host and the mosquito.

☐ Malaria parasites reproduce asexually in the human host, but sexually in the mosquito.

☐ Malaria parasites reproduce asexually in both the human host and the mosquito.

[1]

[Total 2 marks]

2 Sexual and asexual reproduction each have their own advantages and disadvantages. **(Grade 6-7)**

2.1 State **two** advantages of asexual reproduction over sexual reproduction.

....

....

[2]

2.2 An unfavourable environmental change affects a population of organisms.
Explain why sexual reproduction increases the chance of the population surviving.

....

....

....

....

....

[4]

[Total 6 marks]

Topic 6 — Inheritance, Variation and Evolution

X and Y Chromosomes

1 In humans, the biological sex of offspring is determined by a pair of sex chromosomes — X and Y.

Grade 6-7

1.1 Including the sex chromosomes, how many chromosomes are there in a normal body cell?
Tick **one** box.

☐ 22 single chromosomes   ☐ 22 pairs of chromosomes

☐ 23 pairs of chromosomes   ☐ 23 single chromosomes

[1]

Figure 1 shows how the biological sex of offspring is determined.

Figure 1

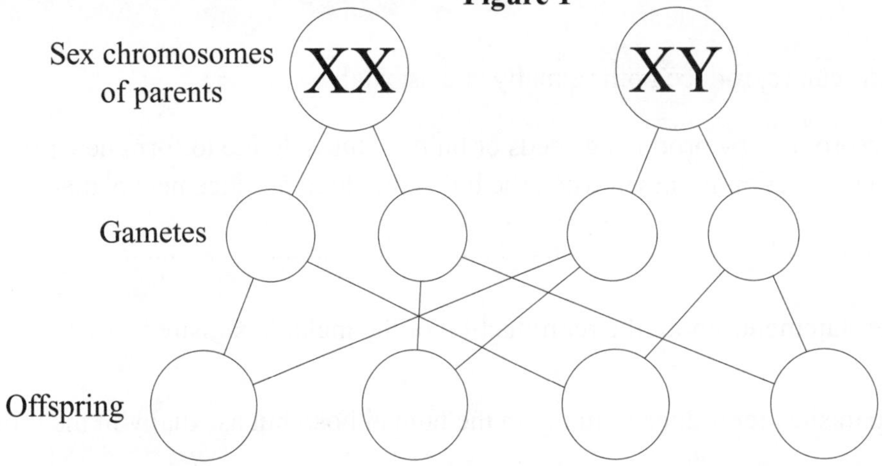

Sex chromosomes of parents: XX   XY

Gametes

Offspring

1.2 Circle the male parent in **Figure 1**.

[1]

1.3 Fill in the sex chromosomes of the gametes produced by each parent in **Figure 1**.

[1]

1.4 Complete **Figure 1** to show the combination of sex chromosomes in the offspring.

[1]

1.5 What is the ratio of male to female offspring?

....

[1]

1.6 Sex determination can also be shown in a Punnett square.
Produce a Punnett square to show how the biological sex of offspring is determined.

[2]

[Total 7 marks]

Exam Tip

If you're asked to draw a Punnett square in the exam, make sure you end up with four single letters outside the square, and four pairs of letters inside the square. Getting just one letter wrong could lose you a mark, so be careful.

Topic 6 — Inheritance, Variation and Evolution

Genetic Diagrams

Use the words and phrases to complete the passage below. You don't have to use every one.

homozygous   dominant   multiple genes   genotypes   homologous
alleles   recessive   heterozygous   a single gene

Genes exist in different versions called .... These can be

dominant or .... If an individual has two copies of the same version

of a gene, they are said to be ...., but if they have two different

versions, they are said to be .... Some characteristics are controlled

by ...., but most are controlled by ....

1   **Figure 1** shows a family tree for the inheritance of a genetic disease.

Figure 1

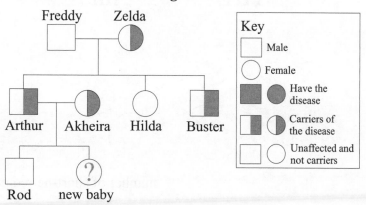

1.1 How can you tell that the allele for the disease is not dominant?

....

....

[1]

1.2 The alleles for the disease are D and d. Both Arthur and Akheira are carriers of the disease.
Complete the Punnett square in **Figure 2** to determine the probability of their new baby
being unaffected and not a carrier of the disease.

Figure 2

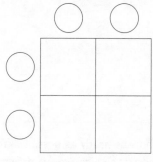

probability = ... %

[4]

[Total 5 marks]

Topic 6 — Inheritance, Variation and Evolution

98

2 Hair length in dogs is controlled by two alleles. Short hair is caused by the allele 'H' and long hair is caused by the allele 'h'. **Figure 3** shows a genetic diagram of a cross between two dogs with the genotype Hh.

Figure 3

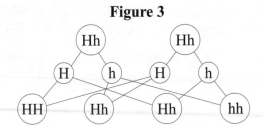

2.1 What is the expected ratio of short-haired puppies to long-haired puppies in this cross?

....

[1]

2.2 A dog with the genotype HH was crossed with a dog with the genotype hh.
They had 8 puppies. How many of those puppies would you expect to have short hair?

Complete **Figure 4** below to explain your answer.

Figure 4

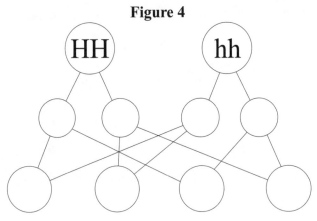

number of short-haired puppies = ...

[3]

2.3 A male dog heterozygous for short hair was then crossed with a female dog homozygous for long hair. What would you expect the ratio of long-haired to short-haired puppies to be in the offspring of this cross?

Construct a Punnett square to explain your answer.

ratio = ...

[3]

[Total 7 marks]

Exam Tip

It's really important that you draw your diagrams as neatly as possible. You could know exactly what it should look like, but if the person marking your paper can't understand what you've drawn they won't be able to give you the marks. So draw it with a pencil and use all the space that you're given. A tiny squiggle in the corner would be tricky to read.

Topic 6 — Inheritance, Variation and Evolution

Inherited Disorders

1 Polydactyly and cystic fibrosis are examples of inherited disorders. (Grade 6-7)

1.1 What are the symptoms of polydactyly?

....

[1]

1.2 A person only has to have one allele for polydactyly to have symptoms.
What does this tell you about the allele that causes polydactyly?

....

[1]

1.3 Even if both parents each carry one copy of the allele that causes cystic fibrosis, there is only
a relatively small chance that their offspring will have the disorder. Explain why this is the case.

....

....

....

[3]

[Total 5 marks]

2 Embryos can be screened for genetic disorders like cystic fibrosis.
The results of screening sometimes results in the embryo being destroyed. (Grade 7-9)
There are lots of arguments for and against embryo screening.

2.1 Suggest **three** arguments against embryo screening.

....

....

....

....

....

....

[3]

2.2 Suggest **three** arguments for embryo screening.

....

....

....

....

....

....

[3]

[Total 6 marks]

Topic 6 — Inheritance, Variation and Evolution

The Work of Mendel

Circle the correct words or phrases below so that the passage is correct.

Gregor Mendel was an Austrian monk who studied mathematics and natural history at the University of Vienna. He is best known for his work on speciation/evolution/<u>genetics</u>. In the <u>late 18th century</u>/early 19th century/mid-19th century, he performed many breeding experiments using <u>fungi</u>/plants/pigs. Mendel noted that offspring often shared characteristics with their parents. He proposed that characteristics were <u>passed on</u>/lost/altered from one generation to the next in units.

1 Scientists didn't realise the importance of Gregor Mendel's research until after his death. **Grade 7-9**

1.1 Suggest why scientists at the time didn't understand how important Mendel's work was.

....

....

....

[1]

1.2 Briefly outline the discoveries made after Mendel's work that built on his discovery of 'hereditary units'. Include how these led to our current understanding of genes.

....

....

....

....

....

....

....

....

....

....

[5]

[Total 6 marks]

Variation

1 Variation occurs in many different organisms. **Grade 4-6**

1.1 Dalmations and pugs are both members of the same species. However, they look very different. For example, dalmations have spots but pugs do not.
What type of variation is causing this difference?

....
[1]

Figure 1 and **Figure 2** show two plants of the same species growing in opposite corners of a garden. The plant in **Figure 1** was grown in a sunny corner, whereas the plant in **Figure 2** was grown in a shady corner.

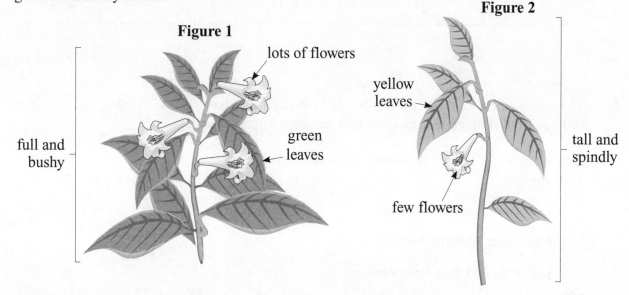

Figure 1

lots of flowers

green leaves

full and bushy

Figure 2

yellow leaves

few flowers

tall and spindly

1.2 What type of variation is causing the differences between the two plants?

....
[1]
[Total 2 marks]

2 Mutations can occasionally lead to a rapid change in a species. **Grade 6-7**
Explain how a mutation could lead to a rapid change in a species.

....

....

....

....
[Total 3 marks]

Exam Tip

Remember that while variation can be caused by either genetic or environmental factors, it's usually caused by a mixture of both interacting with each other. In the exam, you might get an example of variation that you've never heard of before. Don't worry if you do, all the information you need to answer the question will be there. Just apply your knowledge.

Topic 6 — Inheritance, Variation and Evolution

Evolution

1 Evolution by natural selection can sometimes result in the formation of two new species with very different phenotypes.

Grade 4-6

1.1 What is the name of the process by which new species form?

....

[1]

1.2 Explain how you could know for certain if two populations of one original species had become two new species.

....

....

[1]

[Total 2 marks]

2 The theory of evolution is that all species of living things have evolved from simple life forms that first developed many years ago.

Grade 4-6

2.1 How many years ago did the simple life forms develop?
Tick **one** box.

☐ Less than 3 million years ago

☐ More than 3 billion years ago

☐ Less than 300 thousand years ago

☐ More than 5 billion years ago

[1]

2.2 Charles Darwin is best known for proposing the theory of evolution by natural selection.
Some of the evidence that he based his theory on was gathered on his round-the-world trip.
Give **two** other sources of developing knowledge used by Darwin.

....

[2]

When Darwin proposed his theory, he wasn't able to fully explain why everything happened.
Scientists have since been able to use new knowledge of genetics to develop the theory.

2.3 Darwin wasn't able to explain how new variations in phenotype occurred.
What explanation has since been found for new variations in phenotype?

....

[1]

2.4 Darwin was also unable to explain how characteristics are passed on to offspring.
What explanation has since been found for how characteristics are passed on?

....

....

[1]

[Total 5 marks]

3 Extinction is when a species completely dies out because they're not
able to evolve quickly enough to adapt to a change in their environment.
Give **five** factors that can cause a species to become extinct.

....

....

....

....

....

[Total 5 marks]

4 **Figure 1** and **Figure 2** show two hares. The hare in **Figure 1** lives in
a very cold climate. The hare in **Figure 2** lives in a warmer climate.

Figure 1   **Figure 2**

The hare in **Figure 2** uses its large ears as a cooling mechanism. They allow lots
of heat to leave the hare's body. The hare in **Figure 1** has smaller ears.

Suggest how the species of hare in **Figure 1** evolved to have smaller ears than hares that
live in warmer climates.

....

....

....

....

....

....

....

....

....

....

[Total 5 marks]

Exam Tip

In the exam, be careful you don't just rewrite information that you were given in the question — it won't earn you any
extra marks, so it's really just wasting valuable time. For example, in your answer to Q4 above, you don't need to bother
explaining how having big ears will help the hare in Figure 2 cool down, as you were told that in the question.

Topic 6 — Inheritance, Variation and Evolution

More About Evolution

1 When Darwin proposed his theory in 1859, it was highly controversial. (Grade 6-7)

1.1 What was the title of the book in which Charles Darwin proposed his theory of evolution by natural selection? Tick **one** box.

☐ On the Theory of Evolution

☐ On the Origin of Species

☐ On the Process of Natural Selection

☐ On the Progression of Organisms

[1]

1.2 Darwin did not have an explanation for how characteristics were passed on.
Give **two** other reasons why Darwin's theory was controversial at the time it was published.

....

....

....

....

[2]

Other theories on evolution existed at the same time as Darwin's.
One of these was proposed by Jean-Baptise Lamarck.

1.3 What did Lamarck believe about the mechanism of evolution?

....

....

....

[1]

1.4 Lamarck's theory was rejected because experiments didn't support his hypothesis.

Darwin's theory is now widely accepted because lots of evidence supports it, such as the discovery of how characteristics are passed on by genes.

Give **two** other examples of evidence that supports the theory of evolution by natural selection.

....

....

....

....

[2]

[Total 6 marks]

Exam Tip

If you're unsure how much you're expected to write for a question, there are two things you can look at — the number of marks it's worth and how much space you've been given to write. For example, Q1.3 above is only worth one mark, but there are three answer lines — so you should realise you're expected to write more than just a word or a short phrase.

Selective Breeding

1 Selective breeding is used in several different industries. Grade 4-6

1.1 Which of these is another name for the process of selective breeding?
Tick **one** box.

☐ Evolution   ☐ Natural selection   ☐ Inheritance   ☐ Artificial selection

[1]

1.2 What is selective breeding?

....

....
[1]

1.3 Suggest why dairy farmers might use selective breeding.

....
[1]

[Total 3 marks]

2 A dog breeder used selective breeding to produce a litter of puppies that all had a good, gentle temperament. Grade 6-7

2.1* Describe how the breeder could have achieved this, starting from a mixed population of dogs.

....

....

....

....

....

....
[4]

2.2 Suggest why the puppies may be more susceptible to genetic defects.

....

....

....
[2]

2.3 Suggest why a new disease might be an issue for the puppies produced using selective breeding.

....

....

....
[3]

[Total 9 marks]

 ☐   ☐   ☐

Topic 6 — Inheritance, Variation and Evolution

Genetic Engineering

Draw circles to show whether the statements below are **true** or **false**.

Genetic engineering can only be carried out on plants.	True /	False
Genetic engineering has been proven to be 100% risk free.	True /	False
Crops that have been genetically engineered are already being grown.	True /	False
Vectors in genetic engineering can be bacterial plasmids.	True /	False

1   Genetic engineering is being investigated for use in a wide variety of applications. *Grade 6-7*

1.1   What is genetic engineering?

....

....

[2]

The process of genetic engineering has several steps.

1.2   The useful gene is first isolated from an organism's DNA. Explain how this is done.

....

....

[1]

1.3   The gene is then inserted into the target organism's genome.
Explain how this is achieved so that the organism develops with the desired characteristics.

....

....

....

....

[3]

1.4   Scientists are currently investigating the applications of genetic engineering in medicine.
Give **two** examples of how genetic engineering has been used to treat human diseases,
or how it could potentially be used.

....

....

....

....

[2]

[Total 8 marks]

Exam Tip

The issues around genetic engineering are far from simple — not everyone agrees it's a good idea. Whatever your opinion is, before your exam make sure you know the steps involved and be aware of its potential benefits and risks.

Topic 6 — Inheritance, Variation and Evolution

2 Genetic engineering can be used to alter the genes and characteristics of food crops. The resulting crops are known as GM crops.

Grade 6-7

2.1 What does 'GM' stand for when referring to crops that have been genetically engineered?
Tick **one** box.

☐ genetically manufactured ☐ genetically mutated ☐ genetically modelled ☐ genetically modified

[1]

2.2 GM crops are often altered to increase their yield. One way in which this can be achieved in some crops is by modifying their genes to make them produce larger fruit.
Suggest **two** other ways in which a crop plant's genes can be altered to increase its yield.

....

....

[2]

A scientist was researching the effect of a genetic modification on fruit size in a species of plant.
He first grew a normal individual of the species in controlled conditions (Plant 1).
He then measured the circumferences of the 10 largest fruits after a set amount of time.
He repeated these steps with a genetically modified individual from the same species (Plant 2).
Table 1 shows the results.

Table 1

	Fruit Circumference (cm)									
Plant 1	16.4	16.8	15.9	16.2	15.7	16.4	16.3	16.0	15.9	16.0
Plant 2	20.2	20.4	19.8	19.6	20.4	20.6	20.2	19.9	20.1	20.0

2.3 Use the data in **Table 1** to calculate the mean fruit circumference for each plant.

Plant 1 = ... cm   Plant 2 = ... cm

[2]

2.4 Calculate the percentage change in mean fruit circumference between Plant 1 and Plant 2.

..............%

[2]

2.5 Not everyone thinks that GM crops are a good idea.
Give **one** concern that people may have about GM crops.

....

....

[1]

[Total 8 marks]

Cloning

1   Plants can be cloned by tissue culture or by taking cuttings.   (Grade 4-6)

1.1   Which of the following statements is correct?
Tick **one** box.

☐   Taking cuttings is an older and simpler method than tissue culture.

☐   Tissue culture is a newer and simpler method than taking cuttings.

☐   Taking cuttings is a newer and more complicated method than tissue culture.

☐   Tissue culture is an older and more complicated method than taking cuttings.

[1]

Figure 1 shows the process of tissue culture.

Figure 1

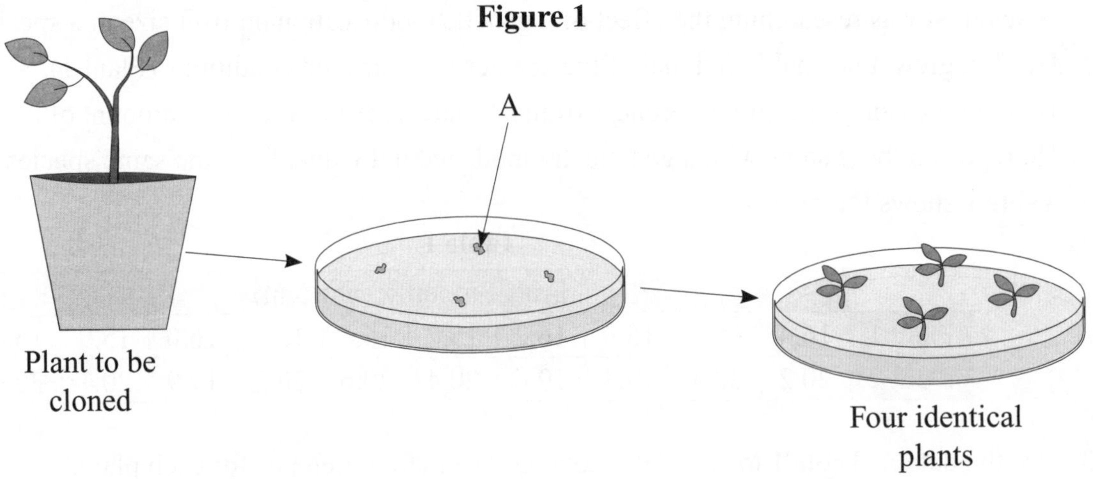

Plant to be cloned

A

Four identical plants

1.2   What is in the Petri dish in **Figure 1**, labelled A?

....

[1]

[Total 2 marks]

2   Plant nurseries sometimes use tissue culture to produce lots of identical plants to sell.   (Grade 6-7)

2.1   Give **one** other use of plant tissue culture.

....

[1]

2.2   Explain a potential risk to plant nurseries of using cloning methods to produce stock.

....

....

....

....

[3]

[Total 4 marks]

Topic 6 — Inheritance, Variation and Evolution

3 Scientists were carrying out some cloning experiments using pigs. **Grade 7-9**

3.1 In one experiment, they wanted to produce a litter of genetically identical piglets using parents with desirable characteristics.
Describe how they could use embryo transplants for this purpose.

....

....

....

....

....

....

....

....

....

[5]

3.2 In another experiment, the scientists wanted to produce an exact clone of a prize-winning pig.
Describe how they could use animal cell cloning in their experiments to clone the pig.

....

....

....

....

....

....

....

....

....

....

....

....

....

[5]

[Total 10 marks]

Exam Tip

Make sure you've got the two different types of animal cloning clear in your head. With all these egg cells and embryos flying around, it's dead easy to get the steps involved in each method jumbled up. Try writing all of the steps for each method down, checking them and then writing them out again. Do this a few times until you can remember every step.

Topic 6 — Inheritance, Variation and Evolution

Fossils

Draw circles to show whether the statements below are **true** or **false**.

Fossils are all between 100 and 1000 years old.	True / False
Fossils are the remains of organisms.	True / False
Fossils are often found in rocks.	True / False

1 The fossil record provides an account of how much different organisms have changed over time. Fossils can be formed in three ways.

1.1 **Figure 1** shows a fossilised insect preserved in amber. Amber is fossilised tree sap. The insect became trapped in the sap as it fed from the tree.

Figure 1

Explain how insects trapped in amber become fossilised rather than decaying.

....

....

[2]

1.2 Describe **two** other ways that fossils are formed.

....

....

....

....

[2]

1.3 Scientists are unable to use the fossil record as conclusive evidence to support or disprove theories on how life on Earth first began. Explain why this is the case.

....

....

....

....

....

....

[3]

[Total 7 marks]

Speciation

1 Alfred Russel Wallace and Charles Darwin were British biologists who carried out work on how species form and evolve. *(Grade 4-6)*

1.1 Alfred Russel Wallace and Charles Darwin proposed that evolution took place by one specific process. What is the name of that process? Tick **one** box.

☐ Normal selection   ☐ Natural Variation   ☐ Natural selection   ☐ Normal variation

[1]

1.2 Which of the following statements is correct? Tick **one** box.

☐ Alfred Russel Wallace published 'On the Origin of Species' in 1859.

☐ Charles Darwin published 'On the Origin of Species' in 1859.

☐ Alfred Russel Wallace published 'On the Origin of Species' in 1851.

☐ Charles Darwin published 'On the Origin of Species' in 1851.

[1]

1.3 Alfred Russel Wallace worked on the theory of speciation.
State **one** other area of research that he was known for.

....

[1]

[Total 3 marks]

2 A population of a species is split up after its habitat is flooded.
Two isolated populations of the species form.
Explain how this could lead to the development of a new species.
Refer to variation and natural selection in your answer. *(Grade 7-9)*

....

....

....

....

....

....

....

....

....

....

[Total 5 marks]

Exam Tip

Sometimes, if a question is worth a lot of marks, it might ask you to talk about more than one thing. You'll need to talk about all the things it asks you for if you want to get full marks, so go back and check that you've covered everything.

 ☐   ☐   ☐

Topic 6 — Inheritance, Variation and Evolution

Antibiotic-Resistant Bacteria

1 Antibiotic resistance in bacteria is becoming an increasing problem in medicine. This is partly due to the overuse of antibiotics.

Grade 4-6

1.1 The overuse of antibiotics is sometimes caused by them being prescribed inappropriately. Give **two** examples of antibiotics being prescribed inappropriately.

....

....

[2]

1.2 Explain why patients prescribed a course of antibiotics should always complete the full course.

....

....

....

[3]

[Total 5 marks]

2 Antibiotic-resistant strains of bacteria are harder to treat because the conventional antibiotics used to kill them are now ineffective. New antibiotics are being developed, but it's unlikely that we'll be able to keep up with the emergence of new resistant strains.

Grade 6-7

2.1 Explain why the development of antibiotics is unlikely to keep up with the emergence of new antibiotic-resistant bacteria.

....

....

[2]

2.2 Explain how antibiotic-resistant strains of bacteria develop and spread.

....

....

....

....

....

....

....

....

....

[5]

[Total 7 marks]

Topic 6 — Inheritance, Variation and Evolution

Target AO3

3 A scientist has samples of two strains of the same species of bacterium, strain A and strain B. This species of bacterium is usually killed by the antibiotic ampicillin, but the scientist believes that strain B may have become resistant to ampicillin.

3.1* The scientist has the following materials and equipment:

> * ampicillin solution
> * samples of bacterial strain A and strain B, growing in nutrient broth solution
> * sterile small glass bottles, with lids
> * sterile nutrient broth solution (culture medium)
> * sterile pipettes of different sizes

The sterile nutrient broth is clear, but turns cloudy when bacteria grow in it.

Write a method that the scientist could use to test his hypothesis using this equipment.

....

....

....

....

....

....

....

....

....

....

....

[6]

3.2 Give **one** reason why it is important that the scientist makes sure that all of the material from the experiment is disposed of safely when it is over.

....

....

[1]

[Total 7 marks]

Exam Tip

You could be asked to write a method for an experiment in your exams. If you are, don't worry. Just think carefully through what you'd need to do if you were actually doing the experiment, and write it all down in a sensible order. Remember to include details of what you would do to make it a fair test — otherwise your results wouldn't be valid.

Topic 6 — Inheritance, Variation and Evolution

Classification

1 Evolutionary trees show how scientists think that organisms are related to each other. **Figure 1** shows the evolutionary tree for species A – K.

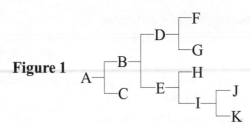

Figure 1

1.1 Give **two** pieces of information that scientists use to prepare evolutionary trees for living and extinct organisms.

....

[2]

1.2 Which species is the most recent common ancestor of species G and species J?

....

[1]

1.3 Which pair of species, G and H or J and K are more distantly related?

....

[1]

[Total 4 marks]

2 Organisms used to be classified into groups using the Linnaean system.

2.1 What is the correct order for the groups of the Linnaean system, from largest to smallest? Tick **one** box.

- [ ] kingdom, phylum, class, order, family, genus, species
- [ ] species, genus, class, phylum, order, family, kingdom
- [ ] kingdom, family, phylum, order, class, genus, species
- [ ] species, class, genus, family, order, phylum, kingdom

[1]

A new classification system, known as the three-domain system, was proposed in the 1990s. In this system, organisms are first divided into domains.

2.2 What is the name of the scientist who proposed the three-domain system?

....

[1]

2.3 Other than fungi, state **three** types of organisms found in the domain Eukaryota.

....

[3]

[Total 5 marks]

> **Exam Tip**
> Evolutionary trees are very handy for figuring out how species are related to each other. If you get given an evolutionary tree in the exam, you could well be asked to interpret it. But don't worry — just keep practising with questions like these.

Competition

1 The plants in a community are often in competition with each other for <u>water</u> and <u>mineral ions</u>.

Grade 4-6

1.1 Where do plants obtain water and mineral ions from?

....

[1]

1.2 Name **two** other factors that plants often compete with each other for.

....

....

[2]

1.3 The animals in a community also compete with each other.
State **three** factors animals compete with each other for.

....

....

....

[3]

[Total 6 marks]

2 Within a community, each species depends on other species for things such as food, shelter, pollination and seed dispersal.

Grade 6-7

2.1 What is this type of relationship called?

....

[1]

Blue tits are relatively common birds that live in woodland communities.
Blue tits feed on caterpillars. Caterpillars live and feed on plants.

2.2 If the caterpillars were removed from the community, suggest what might happen to the numbers of blue tits and plants. Explain your answers.

....

....

....

....

[4]

2.3 Some communities are not stable.
Explain fully what is meant by the term 'stable community'.

....

....

[2]

[Total 7 marks]

Abiotic and Biotic Factors

1   In an ecosystem, there will be both biotic and abiotic factors. *(Grade 4-6)*

1.1   Which of the following statements is correct? Tick **one** box.

☐   Light intensity, temperature and carbon dioxide level are all examples of biotic factors.

☐   Availability of food, carbon dioxide level and pathogens are all examples of abiotic factors.

☐   Light intensity, temperature and carbon dioxide level are all examples of abiotic factors.

☐   Availability of food, light intensity and pathogens are all examples of biotic factors.

[1]

1.2   Suggest **one** abiotic factor that could affect the distribution of animals living in aquatic areas.

....

[1]

1.3   Suggest **two** abiotic factors that could affect the distribution of plants growing in soil.

....

....

[2]

[Total 4 marks]

2   Red squirrels are native to southern Britain. When grey squirrels were introduced into the same area, the number of red squirrels declined. *(Grade 6-7)*

Suggest why the number of red squirrels declined.

....

....

....

[Total 3 marks]

3   Grasses make their own food by photosynthesis. In grassland communities, the grass leaves provide insects with shelter, a place to breed and a source of food. Visiting birds feed on insects. *(Grade 6-7)*

The birds that visit the grassland to feed become infected with a new pathogen that eventually kills them. What would you expect to happen to the number of grass plants? Explain your answer.

....

....

....

....

[Total 3 marks]

Target AO3

4 Herons are carnivorous birds that eat fish such as perch. The sizes of a population of herons and a population of perch in a lake ecosystem were monitored over ten years. The pH of the lake was also monitored over the same time period. The results are shown in **Figures 1** and **2**.

Figure 1

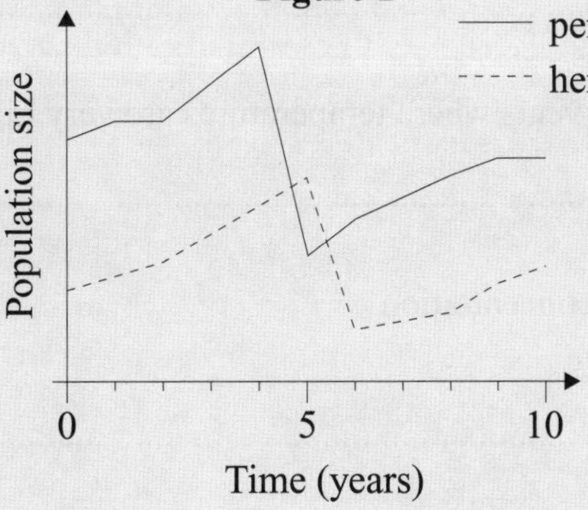

— perch population
--- heron population

Population size / Time (years)

Figure 2

Average pH / Time (years)

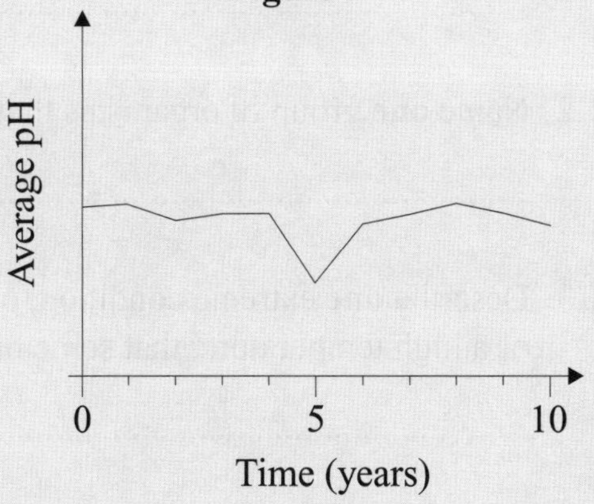

4.1 Describe the trends shown by the two populations in **Figure 1**.

....

....

....

[2]

4.2 Use the data to suggest a reason for the decrease in the perch population between years **4** and **5**. Explain why the data provided cannot be used to confirm what the reason is.

....

....

....

....

[3]

4.3 A new disease has emerged that is predicted to wipe out most of the perch population in the lake. A scientist thinks that the heron population will decrease as a result, because they will lose a source of food. Suggest why the scientist might not be correct.

....

....

....

....

[3]

[Total 8 marks]

Exam Tip

If a question in the exam asks you to use the data, make sure you actually do use the data you're given. It's sitting there in a nice little figure or table, just to help you out, so make the most of it. If you don't use it, you won't get all the marks.

Topic 7 — Ecology

Adaptations

1 Some organisms live in environments that are very extreme, such as environments with a high salt concentration.

Grade 4-6

1.1 What name is given to organisms that live in extreme environments?

....
[1]

1.2 Name **one** group of organisms that can live in deep sea vents where temperatures are very high.

....
[1]

1.3 Describe **one** extreme condition, other than a high salt concentration or a high temperature, that some organisms can tolerate.

....
[1]

[Total 3 marks]

2 Organisms are adapted to the conditions in which they live. **Figure 1** shows a camel and **Figure 2** shows a cactus. Both camels and cacti live in hot, dry desert conditions.

Grade 6-7

Figure 1

long eyelashes

large feet

Figure 2

spines

swollen stem

2.1 Suggest how each of the features in **Figure 1** allow the camel to live in desert conditions.

Long eyelashes ....

....

Large feet...

....
[2]

2.2 Suggest how having spines instead of leaves allows cacti to live in desert conditions.

....
[1]

2.3 Suggest how having a swollen storage stem allows cacti to live in desert conditions.

....
[1]

Cacti can have two types of roots — shallow, wide-spreading roots or long, deep roots.

2.4 For each of these types of root, suggest how the cacti are better adapted to live in desert conditions.

....

....

[2]

[Total 6 marks]

3   Lizards gain most of their heat from the environment. This means that their body temperatures change with the temperature of the environment. **Figure 3** shows a lizard.

Grade
6-7

Figure 3

Lizards control their body temperatures by adapting their behaviour to changes in the environment. For example, in the early morning they lie in the sun to gain heat and only then can they become active.

3.1 Suggest what behavioural adaptation lizards might show when the environmental temperature becomes too hot.

....

[1]

Some lizards also have a structural adaptation that helps them to control their body temperature. They can change the colour of their skin within a range from light to dark. Darker colours absorb more heat than lighter colours.

3.2 Would you expect a lizard in cold conditions to have a dark or light coloured skin?

....

[1]

3.3 There are different types of adaptation, including behavioural and structural. Name **one** other type of adaptation that organisms can have.

....

[1]

[Total 3 marks]

Exam Tip

All of the organisms on these pages are different and have different adaptations to their environment. You could be given information on any organism in the exam but, remember, each feature that the organism has gives it an advantage for living in its environment. You just need to have a think about what that advantage could be. Simple.

Food Chains

On the food chain below, label the producer and the secondary consumer.

seaweed → fish → shark → whale

1   **Figure 1** shows an example of a woodland food chain.

Figure 1

green plants → greenflies → blue tits → sparrow hawk

1.1   What term would be used to describe the greenflies' position in **Figure 1**?

....

[1]

1.2   Green plants produce biomass for the rest of the food chain. Explain how they do this.

....

....

[3]

[Total 4 marks]

2   In a stable community, the numbers of predators and prey rise and fall in cycles as shown in **Figure 2**. In this cycle the predator is a lynx and the prey is a snowshoe hare.

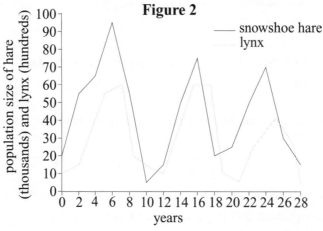

2.1   Describe and explain what happens to the number of lynx between years 4 and 6.

....

....

[2]

2.2   What causes the number of snowshoe hares to fall between years 6 and 10?

....

[1]

[Total 3 marks]

Using Quadrats

1 A group of students used a 0.5 m² quadrat to investigate the number of buttercups growing in a field. They counted the number of buttercups in the quadrat in ten randomly selected places. **Table 1** shows their results.

Grade 7-9

Table 1

Quadrat Number	Number of buttercups
1	15
2	13
3	16
4	23
5	26
6	23
7	13
8	12
9	16
10	13

1.1 Why is it important that the quadrats were placed randomly in the field?

.... *avoid bias* ....

[1]

1.2 What is the modal number of buttercups in **Table 1**?

.... *13* .... buttercups

[1]

1.3 What is the median number of buttercups in **Table 1**?

.... *16* .... buttercups

[1]

1.4 Calculate the mean number of buttercups per 0.5 m² quadrat.

.... *17* .... buttercups per 0.5 m²

[1]

1.5 The total area of the field was 1750 m².
Estimate the number of buttercups in the whole of the field.

175 ÷ ← × 16

2 c

.... buttercups

[3]

[Total 7 marks]

Exam Tip

The mode, median and mean are all different types of average. They all tell you useful, but slightly different, information about the data. Make sure you can remember how to find them all in case one comes up in your exam.

Using Transects

1 A transect was carried out from the edge of a small pond, across a grassy field and into a woodland. The distributions of four species of plant were recorded along the transect, along with the soil moisture and light levels. **Figure 1** shows the results.

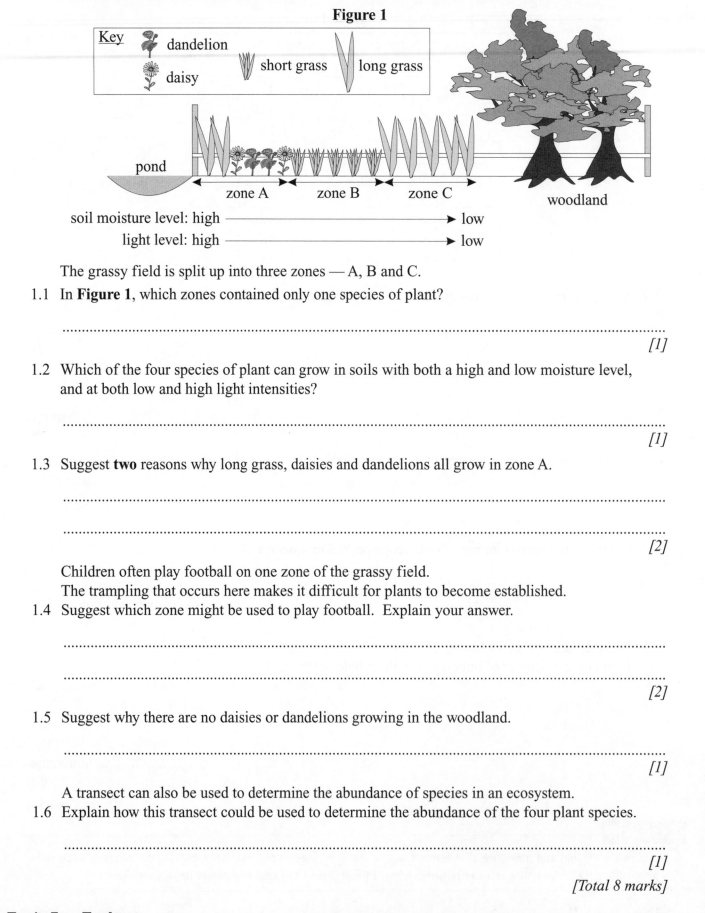

Figure 1

The grassy field is split up into three zones — A, B and C.

1.1 In **Figure 1**, which zones contained only one species of plant?

....

[1]

1.2 Which of the four species of plant can grow in soils with both a high and low moisture level, and at both low and high light intensities?

....

[1]

1.3 Suggest **two** reasons why long grass, daisies and dandelions all grow in zone A.

....

....

[2]

Children often play football on one zone of the grassy field.
The trampling that occurs here makes it difficult for plants to become established.

1.4 Suggest which zone might be used to play football. Explain your answer.

....

....

[2]

1.5 Suggest why there are no daisies or dandelions growing in the woodland.

....

[1]

A transect can also be used to determine the abundance of species in an ecosystem.

1.6 Explain how this transect could be used to determine the abundance of the four plant species.

....

[1]

[Total 8 marks]

2 A group of students are using a transect to investigate the distribution of organisms across a rocky shore.

(Grade 6-7)

PRACTICAL

Figure 2 shows a diagram of the shoreline as seen from above. The students plan to place a quadrat at set intervals along the transect and record the species in the quadrat at each point.

Figure 2

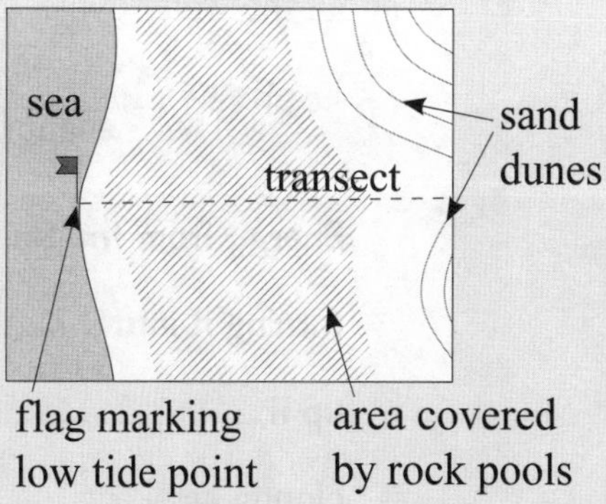

sea

transect

sand dunes

flag marking low tide point

area covered by rock pools

2.1 Suggest one hazard that the students should be aware of while carrying out their investigation.

....

....

[1]

2.2 The students collect their data by placing a 1 m² quadrat at 2 m intervals along the transect and estimating the percentage cover of each organism within the quadrat. Suggest **one** advantage and **one** disadvantage of placing the quadrat at 2 m intervals rather than every metre, with no gap between the intervals.

....

....

....

....

[2]

Table 1 shows the data that the students collected about a seaweed called bladderwrack.

Table 1

Distance from low tide point (m)	2	4	6	8	10	12	14	16	18	20
Percentage cover of bladderwrack in quadrat (%)	0	0	2	10	15	25	40	65	80	75

2.3 Describe the trend in the percentage cover of bladderwrack shown by the data in **Table 1**.

....

....

....

[2]

2.4 The students think that the salt concentration of the water in the rock pools around the bladderwrack affects its growth. Suggest how they could change their method to test this hypothesis.

....

....

[1]

[Total 6 marks]

Exam Tip

If you have time at the end of the exam, have a quick peep back at your answers to make sure that everything you've written is clear and that you've fully answered each question. For example, if you were asked to give advantages and disadvantages for a particular topic, make sure you've written an answer that actually covers both of them.

Environmental Change & The Water Cycle

Warm-Up

Choose from the words below to complete the sentences about the water cycle. Some words may not be used at all.

precipitation   evaporate   warms   cools   water vapour   carbon dioxide   condense

Energy from the Sun makes water .... from the land and sea,

turning it into .... This is carried upwards. When it gets higher

up it .... and condenses to form clouds. Water falls from the

clouds as .... onto land. It then drains into the sea, before the

whole process starts again.

---

1 Lichens grow on the bark of trees. They are sensitive to the concentration of sulfur dioxide in the air, which is given out in vehicle exhaust gases. A road runs by the side of a forest. Scientists recorded the number of lichen species growing on trees in the area. **Figure 1** shows the results.

Figure 1

Number of different species of lichen (y-axis, 0 to 5)
Distance from the main road (m) (x-axis, 0 to 40)

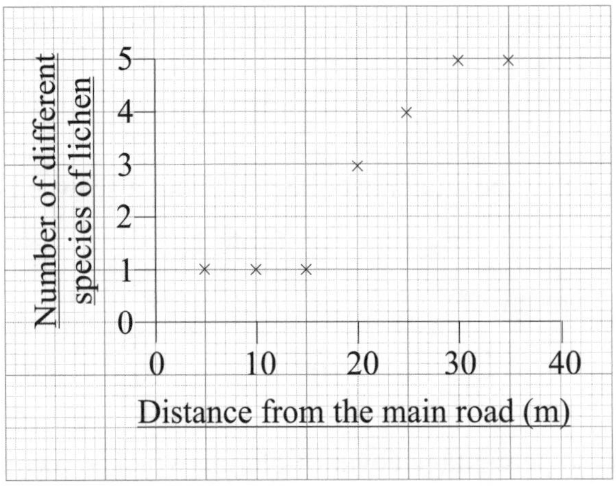

1.1 How many different species of lichen were recorded at 15 m from the main road?

....

[1]

1.2 Describe the relationship between the number of species of lichen growing on the bark of trees and the distance from the main road. Suggest an explanation for your answer.

....

....

[2]

1.3 Based on these results, what is the minimum distance a road should be from a forest to allow at least four species of lichen to grow?

....

[1]

[Total 4 marks]

Topic 7 — Ecology

The Carbon Cycle

1   **Figure 1** shows an unfinished diagram of the carbon cycle.

Figure 1

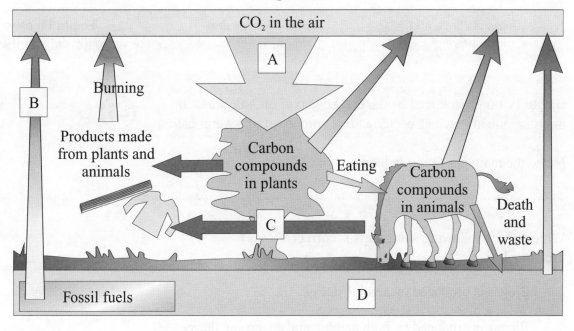

1.1   Name the process represented by **A** in **Figure 1**.

....

[1]

1.2   Which group of organisms remove carbon dioxide from the air?

....

[1]

1.3   Name the process represented by **B** in **Figure 1**.

....

[1]

1.4   Box **C** is the process of changing animal components into products. These can be recycled
to return carbon dioxide to the air. Suggest **one** animal product that can be recycled in this way.

....

[1]

1.5   Process **D** in **Figure 1** is decay. Describe the importance of decay in the carbon cycle.

....

....

[2]

[Total 6 marks]

Exam Tip

In the exam you could be tested on any part of the carbon cycle, so make sure you know the whole of it and not just bits
of it. Try sketching the whole cycle out and make sure you can link each bit together. Don't have your arrows going the
wrong way round, and make sure you understand why the carbon is moving around, e.g. because of respiration. Sorted.

Decay

Circle which household wastes are only made up of organic matter.

| Grass cuttings and food peelings. | Food peelings and empty tin cans. | Empty tin cans and plastic detergent bottles. |

1 Biogas is a fuel produced by the breakdown of organic waste by microorganisms such as bacteria. It is composed of several gases.

Grade 6-7

1.1 Name the main gas found in biogas.

....

[1]

1.2 Which of the following statements is correct?
Tick **one** box.

☐ Biogas is produced by aerobic decay.

☐ Biogas is produced by both aerobic and anaerobic decay.

☐ Biogas is produced by anaerobic decay.

[1]

Biogas is made in a simple fermenter called a generator.

1.3 Biogas generators are often built underground. Suggest **one** reason why.

....

[1]

Gardeners use the breakdown of organic waste to produce compost.

1.4 What do gardeners use compost for?

....

[1]

1.5 Describe **three** conditions that gardeners should use to produce compost quickly.

....

....

....

[3]

[Total 7 marks]

 ☐   ☐   ☐

Investigating Decay

1   A student was investigating the effect of temperature on the decay of milk by an enzyme.

Grade 6-7

1. He added phenolphthalein to a sample of alkaline milk in a test tube and placed it in a water bath.
2. When the mixture in the tube reached the desired temperature, he added some lipase enzyme solution.
3. As the lipase broke down the milk, the pH of the mixture dropped and a colour change occurred.
4. He timed how long it took for the colour change to occur at four different temperatures.
   Table 1 shows his results.

Table 1

Temperature (°C)	Time taken for colour change to occur (s)			
	1st repeat	2nd repeat	3rd repeat	mean
10	292	299	291	294
20	256	257	261	258
30	240	235	239	238
40	217	224	219	

1.1 Phenolphthalein acts as an indicator dye. It is responsible for the visible colour change that occurred. Describe how the colour of the indicator would have changed as pH decreased.

....

[1]

1.2 Calculate the mean time taken for the colour change to occur at 40 °C.

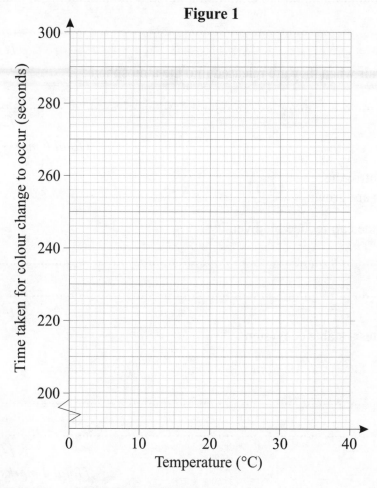

Figure 1

Mean = ... seconds
[1]

Figure 1 is an incomplete graph to show the mean time taken for the colour change to occur against temperature.

1.3 Plot the mean time taken for the colour change to occur at each temperature on **Figure 1**.

[2]

1.4 Complete **Figure 1** by drawing a curve of best fit.

[1]

1.5 Use your curve to predict how many seconds it would take for the colour change to occur at 35 °C.

....

[1]

[Total 6 marks]

Topic 7 — Ecology

Biodiversity and Waste Management

1 Many human activities have an impact on biodiversity. (Grade 4-6)

1.1 Define biodiversity.

....

....

[1]

1.2 Suggest **one** human activity that reduces biodiversity.

....

[1]

[Total 2 marks]

2 The global population is using an increasing amount of resources. (Grade 4-6)

2.1 State **two** reasons why humans are using more resources.

....

....

[2]

If waste is not handled correctly, pollution levels in water and in the air will increase.

2.2 State **two** ways that water can become polluted.

....

....

[2]

2.3 State **two** substances that pollute the air when they are released into the atmosphere.

....

[2]

[Total 6 marks]

3 Herbicides are used by farmers to control the growth of weeds on land where crops are grown. (Grade 6-7)

3.1 Give **two** reasons why using a herbicide can reduce biodiversity.

....

....

[2]

3.2 Explain why a high biodiversity creates a stable ecosystem.

....

....

....

[2]

[Total 4 marks]

Target AO3

4   The presence of indicator species in an area can provide evidence for the level of pollution in the ecosystem. A student is surveying the numbers of three indicator species in two small rivers as a measure of water pollution.

Grade 6-7

This is the method that the student used:

1. Place a long-handled net with a fine mesh on the bottom of the river. It should be positioned so that water is flowing into the net.
2. Stand upstream of the net and gently disturb the bottom of the river by moving your feet for 30 seconds.
3. Empty the contents of the net into a large tray filled with a 3 cm depth of water.
4. Identify and count the individuals of the indicator species in your sample.
5. Empty the contents of the tray back into the river.

Table 1 shows the results. **Table 2** gives details of the indicator species.

Table 1

Individuals counted in survey	River 1	River 2
freshwater shrimp	29	0
water louse	60	10
rat-tailed maggot	4	88

Table 2

Indicator species	Presence of species indicates:
freshwater shrimp	low level of pollution
water louse	medium level of pollution
rat-tailed maggot	high level of pollution

4.1   Use the results to compare the level of water pollution in the two rivers. Explain your answer.

....

....

....

....

[3]

4.2   A factory discharges waste water into River 2 at a site upstream of the sampling site used in the student's survey. A local newspaper claims that the factory discharges are causing an increase in pollution in the river.

Explain how the student's survey would need to change to investigate the newspaper's claim.

....

....

....

....

[3]

[Total 6 marks]

Exam Tip

In your exams, you could be given the method for an experiment and asked how you would need to adapt it to test a different hypothesis. You'll need to have a think about what the original method was testing. Then have a good old read of the new hypothesis you've been given, and work out what things you'd need to change in order to test that.

Topic 7 — Ecology

Global Warming

Fill in the gaps in the passage below using the words on the right.
Not all words need to be used, but each word can only be used once.

The temperature of the Earth is a balance between the energy

it gets from .... and the energy it radiates

back into .... The .... in the

atmosphere act like an insulating layer. They radiate some of

the energy back towards the Earth. This ....

the temperature of the planet.

insulating

the Sun

reflect

increases

the moon   space

gases   decreases

volcanoes

1   Global warming is caused by the increasing
levels of 'greenhouse gases' in the atmosphere.

Grade
6-7

1.1   Which of the following pairs of gases are the main contributors to global warming?
Tick **one** box.

☐ carbon dioxide and sulfur dioxide

☐ carbon dioxide and methane

☐ sulfur dioxide and nitrogen dioxide

☐ nitrogen dioxide and methane

[1]

There are a number of consequences of global warming,
including land becoming flooded.

1.2   Suggest why global warming might cause land to become flooded.

....

....

[2]

1.3   Suggest **two** other consequences of global warming.

....

....

[2]

[Total 5 marks]

Greenhouse gases cause the 'greenhouse effect', but don't get this muddled up with global warming. Without these gases
trapping energy in Earth's atmosphere, it'd be too cold for us to survive. But the increasing amounts of these gases are
increasing the amount of energy being trapped, and that's why we're getting all, ahem, hot and bothered about them.

Deforestation and Land Use

1 State **two** ways in which humans reduce the amount
of land available for other animals and plants.

Grade 4-6

....

....

[Total 2 marks]

2 Peat bogs are sometimes destroyed so that the peat can be burnt as fuel.

Grade 6-7

2.1 Give **one** other reason why peat bogs are destroyed by humans.

....

[1]

2.2 Explain what problem burning peat can cause.

....

....

[2]

2.3 Explain the effect that the destruction of peat bogs has on biodiversity.

....

....

[2]

[Total 5 marks]

3 Biofuel production has caused large-scale deforestation.

Grade 6-7

3.1 Explain why large-scale deforestation has been required to produce biofuels.

....

[1]

3.2 State **two** other reasons for large-scale deforestation.

....

....

[2]

[Total 3 marks]

4 Suggest and explain **two** harmful effects on the environment
caused by the destruction of large areas of trees.

Grade 7-9

....

....

....

....

[Total 4 marks]

Topic 7 — Ecology

Maintaining Ecosystems and Biodiversity

1 In some areas, programmes have been put in place to reduce the negative effects of human activity on ecosystems and biodiversity. *(Grade 4-6)*

1.1 Which of the following would reduce carbon dioxide emissions into the atmosphere? Tick **one** box.

☐ Setting up more breeding programmes for endangered species.

☐ Cutting down large areas of trees for housing development.

☐ Increasing the number of power stations.

☐ Burning fewer fossil fuels.

[1]

1.2 The government encourages people to recycle as much of their waste as possible. Suggest how this could help to protect ecosystems.

....

....

[2]

[Total 3 marks]

2 Monoculture is a form of agriculture in which only one type of crop is grown in a field. *(Grade 6-7)*

2.1 Suggest what effect monoculture has on biodiversity. Explain your answer.

....

....

[2]

2.2 Explain why farmers who grow crops using monoculture may be advised to leave strips of grassland and plant hedgerows around the edges of their crops.

....

[1]

[Total 3 marks]

3 Suggest why some people might be opposed to programmes that maintain biodiversity. *(Grade 7-9)*

....

....

....

....

....

....

....

....

[Total 4 marks]

☹ ☐   ☺ ☐   ☺ ☐

Trophic Levels

The diagram below shows some of the feeding relationships in a rocky shore environment. Sort the organisms into the columns of the table. Each organism belongs in only one column.

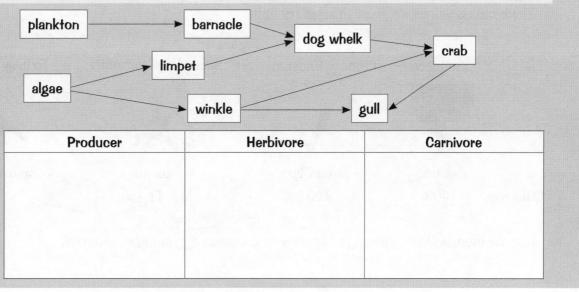

Producer	Herbivore	Carnivore

1 The trophic levels in a food chain can be represented by numbers, starting at level 1 with producers. *(Grade 4-6)*

1.1 Which of the following organisms would be found at level 2? Tick **one** box.

☐ photosynthetic organisms ☐ carnivores ☐ herbivores ☐ decomposers

[1]

1.2 Some carnivores eat other carnivores. Which level represents these carnivores? Tick **one** box.

☐ level 1 ☐ level 2 ☐ level 3 ☐ level 4

[1]

1.3 What is an apex predator?

....

[1]

[Total 3 marks]

2 Decomposers play an important role in ecosystems. *(Grade 6-7)*

Describe their role and explain how they carry it out.

....

....

....

....

[Total 4 marks]

Exam Tip

If you're asked to describe AND explain something in a question then you've got two things to do. First, write down the facts, and then give the reasons for those facts. You'll need to do both things if you want to get the top marks.

 ☐ ☐ ☐

Pyramids of Biomass

1   Pyramids of biomass can be constructed to represent the
relative amount of biomass in each level of a food chain.

Figure 1 shows a food chain from an area of oak woodland.
The biomass values are given in arbitrary units.

Figure 1

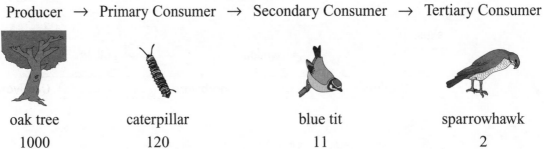

| Producer | → | Primary Consumer | → | Secondary Consumer | → | Tertiary Consumer |

oak tree   caterpillar   blue tit   sparrowhawk

Biomass: 1000   120   11   2

1.1   Use the biomass values given in **Figure 1** to construct a pyramid of biomass.

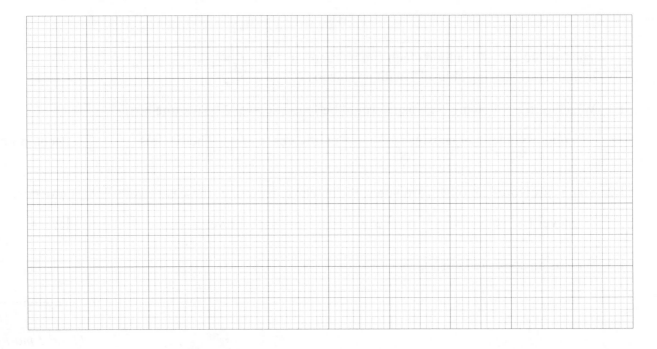

[4]

1.2   Use the biomass values from **Figure 1** to suggest why there are
usually only four or five trophic levels in a food chain.

....

....

[2]

[Total 6 marks]

Target AO3

2 A student wants to estimate the total biomass of dandelions in the school field.

The student writes the following method:

1. Pick a dandelion flower from the field and dry it in an oven for 2 hours.
2. Weigh the dandelion to find the dry biomass of one plant.
3. Place a 1 m² quadrat in several areas of the field where dandelions are visible and record the number of dandelions in the quadrat.
4. Work out the mean number of dandelions in a square metre, then multiply that number by the area of the field.

2.1 The student's teacher points out some errors in her method. The errors are listed below. For each error, suggest how the student could alter her method to avoid the mistake.

The biomass of the whole plant isn't being measured.

....

....

The plant may not be fully dried.

....

....

The sampling isn't representative of the whole field.

....

....

[3]

2.2 The teacher also says that the student should measure the biomass of more than one dandelion and work out the average biomass of a plant.
Give **two** reasons why using a larger sample size could improve the student's investigation.

....

....

[2]

2.3 Dandelions are a source of food for many organisms. Suggest why the student might not want to measure the biomass of a very large number of dandelions from the field.

....

....

[1]

2.4 Suggest **one** potential safety hazard that the student should be aware of while carrying out her investigation.

....

[1]

[Total 7 marks]

Topic 7 — Ecology

Biomass Transfer

1 Not all material that is eaten is used by the body. `Grade 4-6`

1.1 What happens to ingested material that does not get absorbed?

....
[1]

1.2 Name **two** substances lost as waste in urine.

....
[2]

[Total 3 marks]

2 There are losses of biomass at each trophic level in a food chain. `Grade 6-7`

2.1 Explain how respiration affects the amount of biomass
that is transferred from one trophic level to the next.

....

....

....

....
[4]

Table 1 shows the amount of biomass available at each trophic level in a food chain.

Table 1

Trophic Level	1	2	3	4
Biomass available (arbitrary units)	55.30	6.40	0.60	0.06
Efficiency of transfer (%)	–	11.6	X	10.0

The efficiency of biomass transfer between trophic levels can be calculated by using the equation:

$$\text{efficiency} = \frac{\text{biomass transferred to next level}}{\text{biomass available at the previous level}} \times 100$$

2.2 Calculate the value of **X** in **Table 1**.

Efficiency of biomass transfer = ... %
[2]

2.3 Calculate the mean efficiency of biomass transfer between the trophic levels in **Table 1**.

Mean efficiency of biomass transfer = ... %
[2]

[Total 8 marks]

Exam Tip

If you're doing a calculation that has more than one step, pay close attention to what numbers you use in each step and
don't round any numbers until the end. If you round too soon, your final answer could be wrong, losing you marks.

Food Security and Farming

1   Several factors affect food security.   (Grade 4-6)

1.1   Which of the following factors is **not** a threat to food security?
Tick **one** box.

☐   A new disease that affects crops.

☐   Conflict over resources.

☐   Decreasing birth rate.

☐   High costs of farming.

[1]

1.2   Give **one** example of an environmental change that could affect food production.

....

[1]

[Total 2 marks]

2   Fish stocks around the world are monitored regularly.   (Grade 6-7)

2.1   Explain why it is important to maintain fish stocks at a level where breeding continues.

....

[1]

2.2   What has been done to try to conserve fish stocks at a sustainable level?

....

....

....

[2]

[Total 3 marks]

3   Fish can be intensively reared in fish farms, as shown in **Figure 1**.   (Grade 6-7)

Figure 1

3.1   Explain why the movement of fish reared intensively is restricted.

....

....

[2]

Species of fish that are intensively reared include salmon.
Salmon is a carnivorous fish that needs a high-protein diet.

3.2 Suggest why carnivorous species of fish are less efficient to farm than plant-eating fish.

....

....

[2]

3.3 Intensive rearing is also known as 'factory farming'. Animals are kept close together.
Suggest **one** disadvantage of factory farming techniques.

....

[1]

[Total 5 marks]

4 A scientist researched the amount of animal feed needed to produce
1 kg of three different types of meats on a farm. **Table 1** shows the results.

Grade 7-9

Table 1

Animal	Chicken	Pigs	Cattle
Amount of feed needed to produce 1 kg meat (kg)	2.1	4.1	10.5

4.1 Which animal is the most efficient food source? Explain your answer.

....

....

[2]

4.2 Calculate the ratio of the amount of feed needed to produce 1 kg of meat from chicken to the
amount needed to produce 1 kg of meat from cattle. Give the ratio in its simplest form.

Ratio = ... : ....

[1]

4.3 Animals such as cattle, which are farmed for meat, can be fed using crops.
The global production and consumption of meat is increasing.
Suggest what effect increasing meat consumption may have on global food security.
Explain your answer.

....

....

....

....

....

[3]

[Total 6 marks]

Exam Tip

When you're faced with a wordy or difficult-looking question, try underlining the key bits to help you focus on what
is actually being asked (e.g. you could underline the two values that you need to extract from the table in 4.2 above).
By finding the key words, you'll be less likely to mis-read the question or start writing about something totally irrelevant.

Topic 7 — Ecology

Biotechnology

1 Some organisms can be genetically modified to produce desired substances. *Grade 4-6*

1.1 Give **one** use for genetically modified bacteria.

....

[1]

1.2 Suggest **two** advantages of genetically modified crops.

....

....

[2]

[Total 3 marks]

2 Mycoprotein is used to produce protein-rich foods suitable for vegetarians. *Grade 6-7*

2.1 What is the name of the fungus that is used to produce mycoprotein?
Tick **one** box.

☐ *Candida*   ☐ *Fusarium*   ☐ *Penicillium*   ☐ *E. coli*

[1]

The fungus is grown on a culture medium in a fermenter. **Figure 1** shows this process.

Figure 1

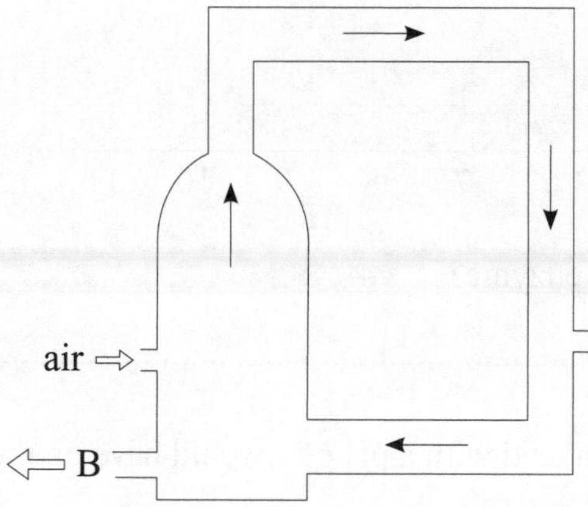

2.2 Which of the following options best describes the conditions in the fermenter?
Tick **one** box.

☐ anaerobic   ☐ aerobic   ☐ both anaerobic and aerobic

[1]

2.3 Substance **A** contains the sugar that the fungus feeds on. Name this sugar.

....

[1]

2.4 Mycoprotein is removed from the fermenter at point **B**.
Suggest the next stage required in the production process.

....

[1]

[Total 4 marks]

😕 ☐   🙂 ☐   😉 ☐

Topic 7 — Ecology

Mixed Questions

1   Alcohol is metabolised in the liver using alcohol dehydrogenase enzymes.   *(Grade 4-6)*

1.1 State **one** function of the liver, other than alcohol metabolism.

....

[1]

1.2 Which of the following sentences about enzymes is **true**? Tick **one** box.

☐ Enzymes speed up chemical reactions in living organisms.

☐ Enzymes are used up in chemical reactions.

☐ Enzymes are products of digestion.

☐ Enzymes are the building blocks of all living organisms.

[1]

A scientist was investigating the effect of pH on the rate of activity of alcohol dehydrogenase. **Figure 1** shows a graph of his results.

Figure 1

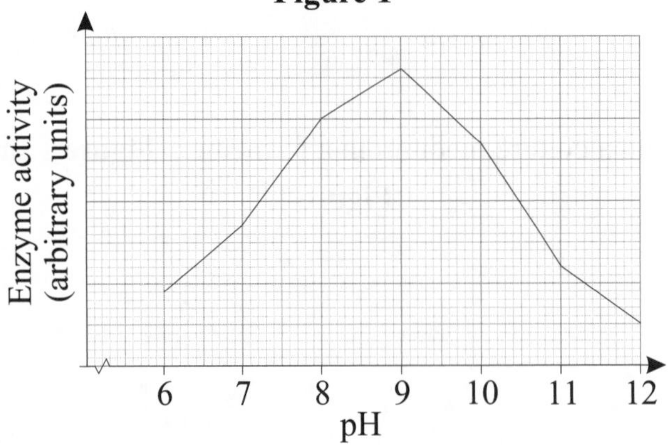

1.3 What is the optimum pH for the enzyme?

....

[1]

1.4 Suggest and explain the effect an acid with a pH of 1 would have on the enzyme.

....

....

....

[3]

1.5 Which of the following statements about alcohol is **not true**? Tick **one** box.

☐ Too much alcohol can cause liver disease.   ☐ Alcohol can cause brain damage.

☐ Alcohol is a risk factor for lung cancer.   ☐ Alcohol can affect unborn babies.

[1]

[Total 7 marks]

Exam Tip

In your exam, you could well get asked to 'suggest and explain' something. In questions like this you're not expected to have studied it already, so just use what you know and apply it to the situation, and then explain what you've suggested.

2 A group of students were investigating the effect of air flow on the rate of transpiration. They set up their apparatus as shown in **Figure 2**.

Figure 2

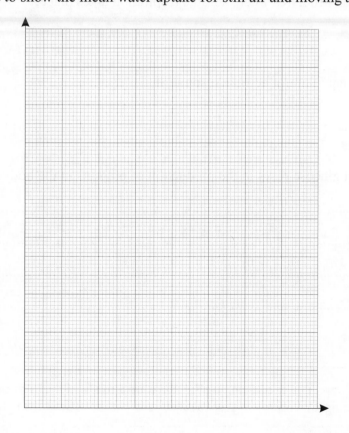

2.1 The tubing and graduated pipette were filled with water.
Suggest why a layer of oil was added to the surface of the water in the pipette.

....

[1]

The students recorded the change in the volume of water in the pipette over 30 minutes, in normal conditions. They repeated this five times. They then carried out these steps with the fan turned on to simulate windy conditions. **Table 1** shows their results.

Table 1

	Repeat	1	2	3	4	5	Mean
Water uptake in	Still Air	1.2	1.2	1.0	0.8	1.1	1.1
30 minutes (cm³)	Moving Air	2.0	1.8	2.3	1.9	1.7	1.9

2.2 Draw a bar chart to show the mean water uptake for still air and moving air.

[2]

2.3 Describe the relationship between air flow around the plant and transpiration rate.

....
[1]

2.4 Explain the effect of air flow on the rate of transpiration.

....

....

....
[2]

2.5 Calculate the range of the results for still air.

Range = ... cm^3
[1]

2.6 The rate of transpiration can be calculated using the formula:

$$\text{rate of transpiration} = \frac{\text{mean volume of water uptake}}{\text{time taken}}$$

Calculate the rate of transpiration for the plant in moving air.
Give your answer in cm^3/hour.

.... cm^3/hour
[2]
[Total 9 marks]

3 Aerobic respiration transfers energy from glucose. **(Grade 6-7)**

3.1 Name the subcellular structures where aerobic respiration takes place.

....
[1]

3.2 Complete the word equation for aerobic respiration.

.... + ... → .... + ...
[2]

3.3 Outline the role that glucose plays in the production of proteins in the body.

....

....

....

....
[3]
[Total 6 marks]

Exam Tip

Before you write your final answer in a calculation question, there are a couple of things to check. Make sure that you've shown your working, put the right numbers into your calculator and put the value in the right units. You've got this.

Mixed Questions

4 The endocrine system uses hormones to produce effects within the body. (Grade 6-7)

4.1 Outline how a hormone travels from a gland to its target organ in the body.

....

....

[2]

The menstrual cycle is controlled by hormones.

Figure 3 shows the change in the levels of these hormones during one menstrual cycle. It also shows the change in the lining of the uterus.

Figure 3

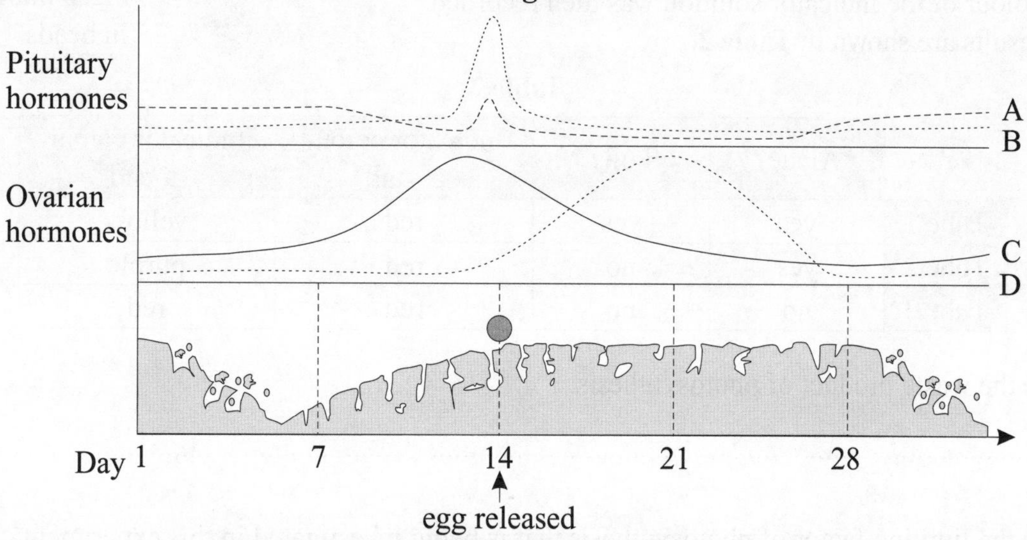

4.2 Which line in **Figure 3** represents oestrogen? Tick **one** box.

☐ A   ☐ B   ☐ C   ☐ D

[1]

4.3 Which line in **Figure 3** represents luteinising hormone? Tick **one** box.

☐ A   ☐ B   ☐ C   ☐ D

[1]

4.4 What is the function of luteinising hormone?

....

[1]

4.5 Where in the body is progesterone produced?

....

[1]

4.6 Taking the combined pill keeps the level of oestrogen in the body constantly high. Explain how this reduces fertility.

....

....

[2]

[Total 8 marks]

5   A student was investigating the effect of limiting factors on the rate of photosynthesis by green algae.

The student set up two boiling tubes as shown in **Figure 4**. She also set up a third tube that did not contain any algae. The colour of the indicator solution changes as follows:

Figure 4

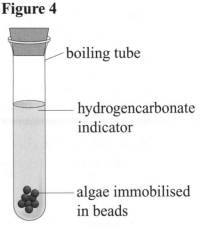

- At atmospheric CO_2 concentration, the indicator is red.
- At low CO_2 concentrations, the indicator is purple.
- At high CO_2 concentrations, the indicator is yellow.

The student covered one of the boiling tubes containing algae with foil. All three tubes were left for several hours at room temperature with a constant light source.
The colour of the indicator solution was then recorded.
The results are shown in **Table 2**.

Table 2

	Algae?	Foil?	Indicator colour at start	Indicator colour at end
Tube 1	yes	yes	red	yellow
Tube 2	yes	no	red	purple
Tube 3	no	no	red	red

5.1 Name the waste product of photosynthesis.

....

[1]

5.2 Name the limiting factor of photosynthesis that is being investigated in this experiment.

....

[1]

5.3 At the end of the experiment, which tube has the highest carbon dioxide concentration?
Tick **one** box.

☐ Tube 1   ☐ Tube 2   ☐ Tube 3

[1]

5.4 Explain the results of Tube 1 and Tube 2.

....

....

....

....

....

[4]

5.5 Give **two** variables that needed to be controlled in this experiment.

....

....

[2]

A scientist investigating the effect of limiting factors on photosynthesis sketched the graph shown in **Figure 5**.

Figure 5

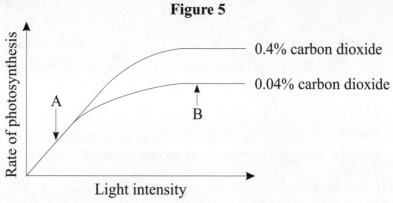

5.6 What is the limiting factor at point **A**? Explain your answer.

....

....

[2]

5.7 Name the limiting factor at point **B**.

....

[1]

[Total 12 marks]

6 In pea plants, seed shape is controlled by a single gene.   (Grade 7-9)

The allele for round seed shape is R and the allele for wrinkled seed shape is r.
R is a dominant allele and r is recessive.

6.1 What is the genotype of a pea plant that is homozygous dominant for seed shape?

....

[1]

6.2 What is the phenotype of a pea plant that is heterozygous for seed shape?

....

[1]

6.3 Two pea plants were crossed. All of the offspring produced had the genotype **Rr**.
Construct a Punnett square to find the genotypes of the parent plants.

Genotypes: .... and ....

[3]

[Total 5 marks]

Exam Tip

Phenotype and genotype are easy words to get mixed up, but they mean very different things. If they crop up in the exam, make sure you're definitely using the right one to answer the question, otherwise you won't get the marks.

7   The life cycle of the protist that causes malaria is shown in **Figure 6**.

Figure 6

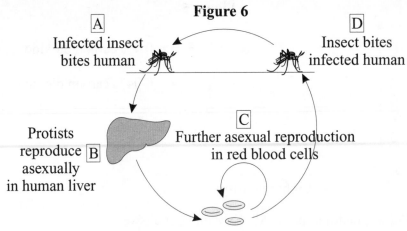

7.1 Suggest **one** method of blocking the protist's life cycle at point **A**.

....

[1]

7.2 Name the type of division that is occurring at point **B**.

....

[1]

7.3 Symptoms of malaria include feeling tired and lacking energy. The protist reproduction at
     point **C** destroys the red blood cells. Explain how this could cause these symptoms of malaria.

....

....

[2]

Malaria can be detected in a blood sample using a diagnostic stick, which works in a similar way
to a pregnancy test. The stick is made from a strip of paper inside a plastic case. At one end of
the stick, the paper contains antibodies (labelled with dye) that are specific to a malaria antigen
— this is where a drop of blood and some colourless flushing agent are added. A positive result is
revealed if a coloured line appears at a point further along the stick, as shown in **Figure 7**.

Figure 7

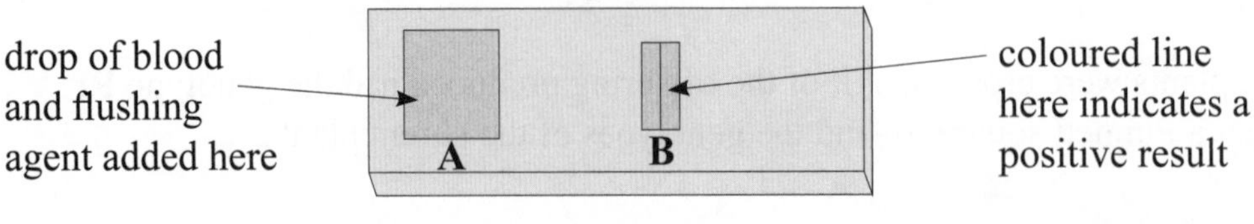

drop of blood
and flushing   coloured line
agent added here   here indicates a
                    A   B   positive result

7.4 Suggest why some flushing agent is added with the blood at point **A** on the diagnostic stick.

....

[1]

7.5 The sample then moves along the stick. Suggest why a coloured line appears at point **B**.

....

....

....

....

[4]

[Total 9 marks]

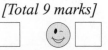

Mixed Questions

Answers

Topic 1 — Cell Biology

Pages 1-2 — Cells

Warm-up

many, plant/animal, animal/plant, single, smaller/ simpler, simpler/smaller

1.1

nucleus

cytoplasm

cell membrane

[1 mark for each correct label]

1.2 Cell membrane — controls what substances go in and out of the cell *[1 mark]*.

Cytoplasm — where most of the chemical reactions take place *[1 mark]*.

Nucleus — controls the activities of the cell / contains genetic material *[1 mark]*.

1.3 E.g. mitochondria *[1 mark]* where aerobic respiration takes place *[1 mark]*, ribosomes *[1 mark]* where protein synthesis occurs *[1 mark]*.

1.4 There is no cell wall/vacuole. / There are no chloroplasts. *[1 mark]*

2.1 bacterium *[1 mark]*

2.2 X – chromosome/DNA/genetic material *[1 mark]*

Y – cell wall *[1 mark]*

Z – plasmid *[1 mark]*

2.3 It contains genetic material *[1 mark]*.

2.4 10 times larger / 1 order of magnitude larger *[1 mark]*

2.5 1 mm × 1000 = 1000 μm

1000 μm ÷ 1 μm = **1000 cells** *[2 marks for the correct answer, otherwise 1 mark for correct working.]*

2.6 E.g. eukaryotic cells have a nucleus, prokaryotic cells do not. / DNA is found inside the nucleus of eukaryotic cells, but is not enclosed in prokaryotic cells. / Prokaryotic cells contain plasmids, eukaryotic cells do not. / Eukaryotic cells have mitochondria, prokaryotic cells do not. *[1 mark]*

Page 3 — Microscopy

1 length of cell A in image = 24 mm

24 ÷ 0.012 = **× 2000** *[2 marks for the correct answer, otherwise 1 mark for correct working.]*

2.1 size of real object = size of image ÷ magnification

actual length = 10 mm ÷ 1000 = **0.01 mm**

[2 marks for correct answer, otherwise 1 mark for correct working.]

2.2 1 mm = 1000 μm

0.01 mm × 1000 = **10 μm** *[1 mark]*

2.3 Electron microscopes have a higher magnification *[1 mark]* and a higher resolution than light microscopes *[1 mark]*.

2.4 E.g. more cell structures can be seen under an electron microscope *[1 mark]* and they can be seen with greater detail *[1 mark]*.

Page 4 — More on Microscopy

1.1 When the specimen is colourless *[1 mark]*.

1.2 × 4 *[1 mark]*

Remember, you should always start with the lowest-powered objective lens — this makes it easier to get your specimen into view.

1.3 They bring the sample into focus by moving the stage up and down *[1 mark]*.

1.4 She should select the × 40 or × 10 objective lens *[1 mark]* and use the adjustment knobs to bring the sample back into focus *[1 mark]*.

1.5 Any two from: e.g. she should use a pencil with a sharp point. / She should make sure her drawing takes up at least half of the space available. / She should not colour or shade her diagram. / She should ensure that the subcellular structures are drawn in proportion. / She should include a title. / She should write down the magnification that it was observed under. / She should label the important features of her drawing using straight, uncrossed lines. *[2 marks]*

Page 5 — Cell Differentiation and Specialisation

Warm-up

root hair cell — Long finger-like projection increases surface area for absorption of water.

xylem — Cells that are hollow in the centre and have no end cell walls form a continuous tube for transporting water from roots to leaves.

phloem — Very few subcellular structures and holes in the end cell walls allow dissolved sugars to move from one cell to the next.

1 differentiation *[1 mark]*

2.1 To fertilise an egg. / To carry the male DNA to the female DNA (in the egg). *[1 mark]*

2.2 E.g. it has a tail to enable it to swim to the egg *[1 mark]*.

It has lots of mitochondria to give it energy *[1 mark]*.

It has a streamlined head to aid swimming *[1 mark]*.

The head contains enzymes to help the sperm penetrate the egg *[1 mark]*.

Page 6 — Chromosomes and Mitosis

1.1

chromosomes

[1 mark]

1.2 DNA *[1 mark]*

1.3 The number of subcellular structures is increasing *[1 mark]*.

The chromosomes are doubling *[1 mark]*.

1.4 The cytoplasm is dividing *[1 mark]*.

The cell membrane is dividing *[1 mark]*.

1.5 They are genetically identical *[1 mark]*.

Answers

Page 7 — Binary Fission

1.1
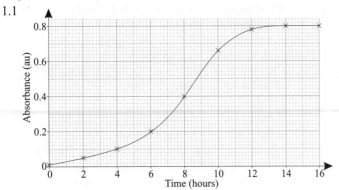

[2 marks for all five points plotted correctly, otherwise 1 mark for 4 points plotted correctly. 1 mark for a suitable curved line of best fit.]

1.2   binary fission *[1 mark]*

1.3   E.g. amount of nutrients / amount of oxygen / build-up of waste *[1 mark]*

2   9 hours = 9 × 60 = 540 minutes

540 ÷ 45 = 12 divisions

2^{12} = 2 × 2 × 2 × 2 × 2 × 2 × 2 × 2 × 2 × 2 × 2 × 2 = 4096 = **4.096 × 10^3**

[4 marks for correct answer, otherwise 1 mark for '540 minutes', 1 mark for '12 divisions' and 1 mark for '4096'.]

Pages 8-9 — Culturing Microorganisms

1.1   Because unwanted microorganisms may have affected the results of the experiment *[1 mark]* and contamination could have resulted in the growth of pathogens *[1 mark]*.

1.2   Any three from: e.g. used sterilised Petri dishes. / Used sterilised culture medium. / Sterilised the spreader/inoculating loop (by passing it through a flame). / (Lightly) taped on the lid of the Petri dish. / Stored the plates upside down. *[3 marks]*

1.3   To reduce the chance of growing harmful pathogens *[1 mark]*.

1.4   10 + 15 + 14 = 39

39 ÷ 3 = **13 mm** *[1 mark]*

1.5   5 mm = 0.5 cm *[1 mark]*

3.14 × 0.5^2 = **0.8 cm^2** *[1 mark]*

1.6
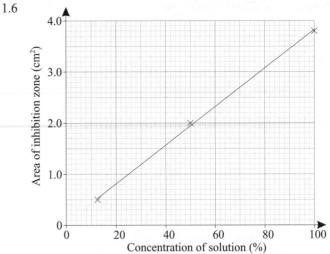

[1 mark for axes with suitable scale and labelled correctly, 1 mark for all points plotted correctly, 1 mark for a suitable straight line of best fit.]

1.7   3.1 cm^2 *[1 mark. Accept answers between 3.0 and 3.2 cm^2.]*

1.8   The higher the concentration of the antiseptic, the more effective it is at preventing bacterial growth *[1 mark]*.

Pages 10-11 — Stem Cells

1.1   meristems *[1 mark]*

1.2   E.g. plants can be produced quickly and cheaply *[1 mark]*. Rare species can be cloned to protect them from extinction *[1 mark]*. Large numbers of identical crop plants with desirable features, e.g. disease resistance, can be grown *[1 mark]*.

2.1   Stem cells can differentiate into many types of body cell *[1 mark]*.

2.2   To increase the number of cells (available for use) *[1 mark]*.

2.3   E.g. because body cells that are already differentiated are not capable of changing into any other types of cell *[1 mark]*.

2.4   E.g. human embryos *[1 mark]*.

2.5   E.g. diabetes / paralysis *[1 mark]*.

2.6   E.g. the cells in the culture medium may become infected with a virus that may then be transferred to the patient *[1 mark]*.

3.1   The production of an embryo with the same genes as a patient *[1 mark]*.

3.2   The stem cells produced by therapeutic cloning won't be rejected by the patient's body *[1 mark]* because they contain the same genes as the patient *[1 mark]*.

3.3   How to grade your answer:

Level 0:   There is no relevant information. *[No marks]*

Level 1:   One or two ethical issues surrounding the use of embryonic stem cells are briefly described, but only one point of view is given. *[1 to 2 marks]*

Level 2:   A detailed discussion of issues surrounding the use of embryonic stem cells is given, including an account of both points of view. *[3 to 4 marks]*

Answers

Here are some points your answer may include:
Some people feel that embryonic stem cells from human embryos shouldn't be used for experiments since each embryo is a potential human life.
Some people may argue that there are other sources of stem cells that scientists could use, so using embryos to create stem cells is unjustified.
Some people think that using embryonic stem cells to cure patients who already exist and who are suffering is more important than the rights of embryos.
Some people argue that many embryonic stem cells are sourced from unwanted embryos from fertility clinics, which would probably be destroyed anyway.

Page 12 — Diffusion

Warm-up

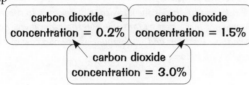

1   protein *[1 mark]*
2.1   The spreading out of particles of a gas *[1 mark]*, resulting in net movement *[1 mark]* from an area of higher concentration to an area of lower concentration *[1 mark]*.
2.2   Increasing the concentration of ammonia increases the rate of diffusion *[1 mark]*.
2.3   Any two from: e.g. the surface area of the cell. / The temperature. / The distance for diffusion. / The permeability of the membrane. *[2 marks]*
2.4   By repeating the experiment and calculating a mean *[1 mark]*.

Pages 13-14 — Osmosis

1.1   The movement of water molecules *[1 mark]* across a partially permeable membrane *[1 mark]* from a region of higher water concentration (a dilute solution) to a region of lower water concentration (a more concentrated solution) *[1 mark]*.
1.2   A plant is absorbing water from the soil *[1 mark]*.
2.1   So that all the pieces of potato have the same water concentration. / Because different potatoes will have different water concentrations. *[1 mark]*
2.2 $\dfrac{(6.58 - 5.73)}{5.73} \times 100$

       = **14.8 %** (3 s.f.) *[2 marks for the correct answer, otherwise 1 mark for correct working.]*
2.3   E.g. 4% *[1 mark. Accept a percentage between 2% and 5%.]*
3.1   Any two from: e.g. the volume of sucrose solution the student puts in the Visking tubing. / The volume of sucrose solution the student puts in the beaker. / The temperature the beaker is kept at. / The size of the Visking tubing bag *[2 marks]*.

3.2   It will stay the same *[1 mark]*. The water concentration of the solution in the tubing is the same as the water concentration of the solution in the beaker, so there will be no net movement of water molecules *[1 mark]*.
3.3   E.g. at first, the level of the solution in the beaker will gradually increase *[1 mark]*. The water concentration of the solution in the tubing is greater than the water concentration of the solution in the beaker, so there will be a net movement of water molecules out of the tubing *[1 mark]*. Later, the level of the solution in the beaker will stop changing *[1 mark]*. The water concentration of the solutions in the tubing and the beaker will have become the same, so there will be no net movement of water molecules *[1 mark]*.

Page 15 — Active Transport

1.1   The movement of a substance from a more dilute solution to a more concentrated solution (against a concentration gradient) *[1 mark]*.
1.2   For energy/respiration *[1 mark]*.
1.3   It needs energy from respiration *[1 mark]*.
2.1   For growth *[1 mark]*.
2.2   The concentration of minerals is higher inside the plant cells than in the soil (outside the plant cells) *[1 mark]* so the minerals would move out of the plant cells by diffusion *[1 mark]*.
2.3   Active transport occurs against a concentration gradient but diffusion occurs down a concentration gradient *[1 mark]*. Active transport needs energy from respiration but diffusion doesn't *[1 mark]*.
2.4   The function of root hair cells is to take up substances from the soil *[1 mark]*. Root hair cells have elongated 'hairs' that stick out into the soil *[1 mark]*. These 'hairs' give the root a large surface area for absorbing substances *[1 mark]*.

Page 16 — Exchange Surfaces

Warm-up
    1 — blue whale, 2 — tiger, 3 — domestic cat,
    4 — bacterium
1   A large surface area. / A thin membrane. / An efficient blood supply. / Being ventilated. *[4 marks]*
2.1   X = (3 × 3) × 6 = **54 cm²** *[1 mark]*
       Y = 3 × 3 × 3 = **27 cm³** *[1 mark]*
2.2   Z = 150 ÷ 125 = **1.2** *[1 mark]*
2.3   5 × 5 × 5, because it has the smallest surface area to volume ratio / it has the most volume for the least surface area / it has the longest diffusion distance to the centre *[1 mark]*.

Page 17 — Exchanging Substances

1.1   A = carbon dioxide *[1 mark]*
       B = oxygen *[1 mark]*
1.2   diffusion *[1 mark]*
1.3   short diffusion pathway — the walls of the alveoli are thin/one cell thick *[1 mark]*
       large surface area — lots of alveoli *[1 mark]*

Answers

2   As the walls of the alveoli are broken down, the surface area in the lungs is reduced *[1 mark]*, so the amount of oxygen that can diffuse into the blood (from the air in the alveoli) at any one time is reduced *[1 mark]*. This means that their body cells are not getting enough oxygen for respiration during exercise, which results in lower energy levels *[1 mark]*.

3   The small intestine is covered in villi *[1 mark]* which increases the surface area for absorption *[1 mark]*. There is a good blood supply *[1 mark]* which maintains the concentration gradient so absorption can happen quickly *[1 mark]*. The villi have a single layer of surface cells *[1 mark]* which give a short diffusion pathway *[1 mark]*.

Page 18 — More on Exchanging Substances
1.1   stomata *[1 mark]*
1.2   Carbon dioxide diffuses into the leaf *[1 mark]*. Water vapour diffuses out of the leaf *[1 mark]*. Oxygen diffuses out of the leaf *[1 mark]*.
1.3   They increase the surface area for carbon dioxide to diffuse into the cells *[1 mark]*.
2.1   They increase the surface area *[1 mark]*.
2.2   To (further) increase the surface area of the gills *[1 mark]*.
2.3   A good blood supply *[1 mark]*.
2.4   A fast-moving fish has more, longer gill filaments than a slow-moving fish. / A slow-moving fish has fewer, shorter gill filaments than a fast-moving fish. *[1 mark]*
2.5   Fast-moving fish are more active than slow-moving fish / Fast-moving fish do more respiration than slow-moving fish *[1 mark]* so they require more oxygen *[1 mark]*.

Topic 2 — Organisation

Page 19 — Cell Organisation
Warm-up
     Organ system – 4, Tissue – 2, Cell – 1, Organ – 3
1.1   X = Liver *[1 mark]*
       Y = Large intestine *[1 mark]*
       Z = Small intestine *[1 mark]*
1.2   A group of organs working together to perform a particular function *[1 mark]*.
1.3   A group of similar cells that work together to carry out a particular function *[1 mark]*.
1.4   It breaks down and absorbs food *[1 mark]*.
1.5   A group of different tissues that work together to perform a certain function *[1 mark]*.

Page 20 — Enzymes
1.1   active site *[1 mark]*
1.2   Part X/the active site is where the substrate involved in the reaction fits *[1 mark]*.
2.1   Line 2 *[1 mark]*
2.2   Line 2 shows an enzyme with a higher optimum temperature than the enzyme shown by Line 1 *[1 mark]* and it doesn't denature until a higher temperature *[1 mark]*. This suggests that the enzyme is adapted to working at the higher temperatures of a thermal vent than the enzyme represented by Line 1 *[1 mark]*.
2.3   The enzyme has been denatured *[1 mark]*, which has changed the shape of its active site *[1 mark]*. This means that the substrate will no longer fit the active site *[1 mark]*, so the enzyme will no longer catalyse the reaction *[1 mark]*.

Question 2 asks you to apply your knowledge of enzymes to a context you've probably not met before. Don't panic in the exam if you get questions like this. Just stop and think about what you know about enzymes, and it'll all become clear.

Page 21 — Investigating Enzymatic Reactions
1.1   pH 6 as this was the pH at which the iodine solution stopped turning blue-black first *[1 mark]*, meaning the starch had been broken down the fastest *[1 mark]*.
1.2   E.g. the amylase was denatured by the high pH, so the starch was not broken down *[1 mark]*.
1.3   By putting the test tubes in a water bath *[1 mark]*.
1.4   Any two from: e.g. the concentration of starch solution / the concentration of amylase / the volume of starch and amylase solution added to the iodine / the volume of iodine solution in the wells *[2 marks]*.
1.5   E.g. test the solutions more frequently (e.g. every 10 seconds) *[1 mark]*.

Pages 22-23 — Enzymes and Digestion
Warm-up

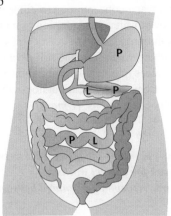

1.1   Carbohydrases *[1 mark]*
1.2   Sugars *[1 mark]*

Answers

2.1 They break down big molecules from food into smaller, soluble molecules that can pass easily through the walls of the digestive system *[1 mark]*, allowing them to be absorbed into the bloodstream *[1 mark]*.

2.2 Any two from: to make new carbohydrates. / To make new proteins. / To make new lipids. / Some glucose is used in respiration *[2 marks]*.

3.1 Produced: liver *[1 mark]*
Stored: gall bladder *[1 mark]*

3.2 It neutralises the acid from the stomach in the small intestine and makes the conditions in the small intestine alkaline *[1 mark]*. This is important because the enzymes in the small intestine work best in these conditions *[1 mark]*. It emulsifies fat *[1 mark]*, which increases the surface area of fat for the enzyme lipase to work on, which makes its digestion faster *[1 mark]*.

4 How to grade your answer:
Level 0: There is no relevant information. *[No marks]*
Level 1: There is a brief description which includes the names of one or more of the relevant enzymes or where in the body they are produced. *[1 to 2 marks]*
Level 2: There is some description of how one or more of carbohydrates, proteins or lipids are digested, including where in the body the relevant enzymes are produced. *[3 to 4 marks]*
Level 3: There is a clear and detailed description of how carbohydrates, proteins and lipids are digested, including reference to where in the body the relevant enzymes are produced and to the end products of the reactions. *[5 to 6 marks]*

Here are some points your answer may include:
Carbohydrate digestion begins in the mouth, where amylase is produced by the salivary glands.
Carbohydrate digestion also occurs in the small intestine, which produces its own supply of amylase and also contains amylase produced by the pancreas.
Amylase converts the carbohydrates into sugars.
Protein is digested in the stomach, where proteases are produced.
Protein digestion also occurs in the small intestine, which produces proteases and also contains proteases produced by the pancreas.
Proteases convert protein into amino acids.
Lipids are digested in the small intestine, which produces lipases and also contains lipases produced by the pancreas.
Lipases convert lipids to fatty acids and glycerol.
The products of the digestive enzymes are absorbed into the bloodstream.

Page 24 — Food Tests

Warm-up
Biuret test — Proteins, Benedict's test — Reducing sugars, Sudan III test — Lipids, Iodine test — Starch

1 How to grade your answer:
Level 0: There is no relevant information. *[No marks]*
Level 1: There is a brief description of how to carry out the investigation. *[1 to 2 marks]*
Level 2: There is some description of how to carry out the investigation but some details are missing. *[3 to 4 marks]*
Level 3: There is a clear and detailed description of how to carry out the investigation. *[5 to 6 marks]*

Here are some points your answer may include:
Grind up a sample of the egg white using a pestle and mortar.
Put the sample into a beaker and add some distilled water.
Stir well with a glass rod to allow some of the food to dissolve in the water.
Filter the mixture through a funnel lined with filter paper.
Transfer 2 cm^3 of the filtered solution into a clean test tube.
Add 2 cm^3 of Biuret solution and gently shake the test tube.
If the food sample contains protein, the solution will change from blue to purple.
If no protein is present, the solution will stay bright blue.

2.1 He should add some Benedict's solution to each test tube using a pipette *[1 mark]*. He should then place the test tubes in a water bath set at 75 °C and leave them for 5 minutes *[1 mark]*. He should look out for a colour change and note which of a range of colours the solutions become *[1 mark]*.

Glucose is a reducing sugar so the Benedict's test can be used to determine the relative concentrations of glucose in the test tubes.

2.2

	Tube 1	Tube 2	Tube 3	Tube 4
substance observed	yellow precipitate	blue solution	red precipitate	green precipitate
glucose concentration (M)	**0.1**	**0**	**1**	**0.02**

[1 mark]

The higher the concentration of glucose in the solution, the further the colour change goes along the following scale: blue — green — yellow — brick red. If no precipitate forms then there are no reducing sugars in the solution.

Page 25 — The Lungs

Warm-up
bronchi, alveoli, oxygenates, carbon dioxide

1.1 A = trachea *[1 mark]*
B = bronchus *[1 mark]*
C = alveolus/alveoli *[1 mark]*

1.2 capillary *[1 mark]*

Answers

1.3 The capillary carries blood that is returning from the rest of the body and contains a higher concentration of carbon dioxide than in the lungs *[1 mark]*. The carbon dioxide diffuses into the alveoli, where there is a lower concentration, to be breathed out *[1 mark]*. The capillary also picks up oxygen from the alveoli, which contain a higher concentration of oxygen than in the blood *[1 mark]*. Oxygen diffuses from the alveoli into the blood, where there is a lower concentration, to be carried to the body cells *[1 mark]*.

Page 26 — Circulatory System — The Heart

1.1 X = aorta *[1 mark]*
Y = pulmonary vein *[1 mark]*
Z = (right) ventricle *[1 mark]*

1.2

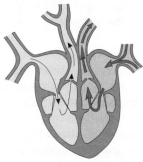

[1 mark for arrow(s) showing blood flow from the vena cava, through the right atrium and ventricle, then up through the pulmonary artery.]

1.3 Because it consists of two circuits joined together *[1 mark]*. The first one pumps deoxygenated blood to the lungs to take in oxygen and returns oxygenated blood to the heart *[1 mark]*. The second one pumps oxygenated blood around all the other organs of the body and returns deoxygenated blood to the heart *[1 mark]*.

2.1 The heartbeat is controlled by a group of cells in the right atrium wall *[1 mark]* that act as a pacemaker *[1 mark]*.

2.2 An artificial pacemaker could be fitted *[1 mark]*. This produces an electric current to keep the heart beating regularly *[1 mark]*.

Pages 27-28 — Circulatory System — Blood Vessels

1.1 A *[1 mark]*

1.2 The walls of arteries contain thick layers of muscle to make them strong *[1 mark]* and elastic fibres to allow them to stretch and spring back *[1 mark]*.

1.3 veins *[1 mark]*

1.4 To prevent the blood flowing backwards / to keep the blood flowing in the right direction *[1 mark]*.

1.5 Capillaries carry blood close to cells to exchange substances with them *[1 mark]*. Having thin walls increases the rate at which substances can diffuse across them by decreasing the distance over which diffusion occurs *[1 mark]*.

2.1 E.g. the graph shows that as an increasing amount of mass was added and then removed from the ring of artery, the percentage change in the ring's length remained at 0 *[1 mark]*, so the ring returned to its original length each time the mass was removed *[1 mark]*. As the amount of mass added and then removed from the ring of vein increased, the percentage change in the ring's length increased *[1 mark]*, so the ring did not return to its original length once the mass was removed and the greater the mass, the further it was from its original length *[1 mark]*.

2.2 Any sensible precaution, e.g. wear safety goggles / wear gloves / disinfect the workstation after the experiment / wash hands after the experiment *[1 mark]*.

Page 29 — Circulatory System — Blood

1.1 Because white blood cells defend against infection *[1 mark]*.

1.2 Some white blood cells can change shape to engulf microorganisms in a process called phagocytosis *[1 mark]*. Others produce antibodies to fight microorganisms *[1 mark]* or antitoxins to neutralise any toxins produced by the microorganisms *[1 mark]*.

1.3 They have a biconcave disc shape to give a large surface area for absorbing oxygen *[1 mark]*. They don't have a nucleus, which allows more room to carry oxygen *[1 mark]*. They contain haemoglobin, which binds to oxygen and transports it to cells in the body tissues *[1 mark]*.

1.4 plasma *[1 mark]*

1.5 Platelets are small fragments of cells with no nucleus *[1 mark]*. They help the blood to clot at a wound *[1 mark]*.

Pages 30-31 — Cardiovascular Disease

Warm-up

blood vessels, coronary heart disease, coronary arteries, fatty material

1.1 Because it restricts the blood flow to the heart muscle *[1 mark]*, leading to a lack of oxygen reaching it *[1 mark]*.

1.2 The doctor might recommend a stent *[1 mark]*. Stents are tubes that are inserted inside arteries to keep them open to make sure that blood can pass through to the heart muscle *[1 mark]*.

2.1 They reduce the amount of 'bad' cholesterol present in the bloodstream *[1 mark]*. This slows down the rate of fatty deposits forming in the coronary arteries *[1 mark]*.

2.2 E.g. he is worried about side effects the statins might cause *[1 mark]*.

3.1 It would allow the blood to flow in both directions in part of the heart *[1 mark]*, meaning that blood doesn't circulate around the body as effectively as normal *[1 mark]*.

3.2 It might not open fully *[1 mark]*.

3.3 A valve taken from a human or another mammal *[1 mark]*.

3.4 A man-made/artificial valve *[1 mark]*.

Answers

3.5 To keep a patient alive while waiting for a donor heart to be found *[1 mark]* or to help a person recover by allowing their heart to rest and heal *[1 mark]*.

3.6 Advantage — e.g. natural donor hearts don't have any mechanical parts like electric motors that could wear out. / Blood flows more smoothly through natural hearts *[1 mark]*.
Disadvantage — e.g. natural donor hearts aren't always available straight away. / Natural donor hearts are more likely to be rejected by the body's immune system *[1 mark]*.

Page 32 — Health and Disease

1.1 A disease that can spread from person to person or between animals and people *[1 mark]*.

1.2 Any two from: whether you have a good, balanced diet. / The stress you are under. / Your life situation *[2 marks]*.

2.1

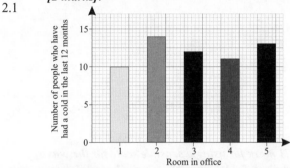

[1 mark for each correctly drawn bar for rooms 3 and 5.]

Room 1	Room 2	Room 3	Room 4	Room 5	Total
10	**14**	12	11	**13**	60

[1 mark for each number filled in correctly.]
You're given the total number of people who have had colds in the table (60). So to work out the figure for Room 5, you'd take the total for Rooms 1–4 away from 60.

2.2 It would increase the chance of the person getting a communicable disease *[1 mark]* because their body is less likely to be able to defend itself against the pathogen that causes the disease *[1 mark]*.

Pages 33-34 — Risk Factors for Non-Communicable Diseases

1.1 Something that is linked to an increase in the likelihood that a person will develop a certain disease during their lifetime *[1 mark]*.

1.2 Aspects of a person's lifestyle *[1 mark]*.
Substances in the body *[1 mark]*.

1.3 E.g. type 2 diabetes *[1 mark]*.

2.1 Any two from: e.g. a high fat diet / a lack of exercise / smoking *[2 marks]*.

2.2 Any two from: e.g. the cost of researching and treating non-communicable diseases is huge. / Families may have to move or adapt their home to help a family member with a non-communicable disease, which can be costly. / If someone has to give up work or dies because of a non-communicable disease, family income will be reduced. / A reduction in the number of people able to work may affect a country's economy *[2 marks]*.

3.1 The number of people with diabetes increased between 2012 and 2018 *[1 mark]*.

3.2 How to grade your answer:
Level 0: There is no relevant information. *[No marks]*
Level 1: One or two comments about the student's statements are made but only points in support of or against the student's statement are given. *[1 to 2 marks]*
Level 2: A detailed discussion of the student's statement is given, including points both in support and against. *[3 to 4 marks]*
Here are some points your answer may include:
In support of the student's statement:
Both graphs show an overall positive correlation. / Both the rate of obesity and the rate of diabetes increase overall between 2012 and 2018.
It is generally accepted that obesity is a risk factor for Type 2 diabetes.
Against the student's statement:
A correlation between the number of people with diabetes and the prevalence of obesity doesn't show that diabetes is caused by obesity — there may be another factor that affects both.
Figure 1 shows that the percentage of people with obesity fell between 2015 and 2016, while the number of people with diabetes increased in the same year, which contradicts the student's statement.
The student is only comparing data for seven years — it may be that the trend is not present over a longer period of time.

Page 35 — Cancer

Warm-up

Malignant Tumours — Are cancerous
Benign Tumours — Are not cancerous
— Can invade neighbouring tissues

1.1 Uncontrolled cell division *[1 mark]*

1.2 E.g. genetic risk factors *[1 mark]*

2.1 malignant *[1 mark]*

2.2 Cells break off a tumour and spread to other parts of the body by travelling in the bloodstream *[1 mark]*.
The malignant cells then invade healthy tissues elsewhere in the body and form secondary tumours *[1 mark]*.

Answers

Page 36 — Plant Cell Organisation

1.1 An organ system *[1 mark]*

1.2 Water *[1 mark]*, mineral ions *[1 mark]*

2.1 Growing tips of roots *[1 mark]*
Growing tips of shoots *[1 mark]*

2.2 It can differentiate into lots of different types of plant cells *[1 mark]*.

3.1 A: palisade mesophyll tissue *[1 mark]*
B: spongy mesophyll tissue *[1 mark]*

3.2 It contains lots of chloroplasts, which are the structures where photosynthesis takes place *[1 mark]* and is located near the top of the leaf so that the chloroplasts can get the most light *[1 mark]*.

3.3 They increase the rate of diffusion of gases *[1 mark]*.

Page 37 — Transpiration and Translocation

Warm-up

transpiration, evaporation, leaves, translocation, sugars, phloem

1 How to grade your answer:

Level 0: There is no relevant information. *[No marks]*

Level 1: There is a brief description of either the structure or the function of one or both of the plant tissues. *[1 to 2 marks]*

Level 2: There is some description of both the structure and the function of both plant tissues. *[3 to 4 marks]*

Level 3: There is detailed description of both the structure and the function of both plant tissues. *[5 to 6 marks]*

Here are some points your answer may include:
Xylem is made of dead cells joined together end to end.
The walls are strengthened with lignin.
The dead cells have no end walls between them, so there is a hole down the middle of the tissue.
Water and mineral ions travel through the xylem tubes from the roots to the stem and leaves.
This is called the transpiration stream.
Phloem is made of columns of elongated living cells.
The cells have small pores in the end walls to allow cell sap to flow through.
This means that dissolved sugars made in the leaves can travel to the rest of the plant.
Phloem can transport dissolved sugars in both directions in the tissue.
Transport of dissolved sugars in phloem is called translocation.

Pages 38-39 — Transpiration and Stomata

1.1 X = stomata *[1 mark]*
Y = guard cells *[1 mark]*

1.2 They are responsible for opening and closing the stomata *[1 mark]* in order to control gas exchange and water loss from a leaf *[1 mark]*.

2.1 Mean width of stomata in leaf A =
(25.2 + 20.1 + 18.7 + 17.9 + 19.1 + 19.3 + 22.0 + 23.1 + 21.8 + 20.3) ÷ 10 = **20.8 μm** *[1 mark]*

Mean width of stomata in leaf B =
(14.7 + 12.8 + 14.1 + 13.2 + 12.9 + 11.9 + 12.1 + 13.4 + 10.9 + 11.7) ÷ 10 = **12.8 μm** *[1 mark]*

2.2 Leaf B *[1 mark]*

2.3 Because stomata begin to close when it gets darker / Less carbon dioxide is needed for photosynthesis at lower light intensities *[1 mark]* and so the leaf with the lower mean will have had the measurements taken in a lower light intensity *[1 mark]*.

3.1

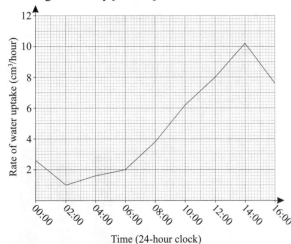

[1 mark for using a sensible scale for the y-axis, 1 mark for labelling the y-axis, 1 mark for accurately plotting the points, 1 mark for connecting the points with straight lines through the centre of each point.]

It might sound a bit obvious, but make sure you always use a sharp pencil to draw graphs like this. Your graph might turn out inaccurate if your pencil is blunt, which could lose you marks.

3.2 5.0 cm³/hour *[1 mark]*

3.3 5.1 cm³/hour *[1 mark]*

3.4 Any two from: e.g. light intensity increased. / Temperature increased. / Air flow around the leaf improved. / Humidity decreased *[2 marks]*.

Topic 3 — Infection and Response

Page 40 — Communicable Disease

1.1 Both bacteria and viruses can reproduce quickly in the body *[1 mark]*.

1.2 It can cause the cells to burst *[1 mark]*.

2 How to grade your answer:

Level 0: There is no relevant information. *[No marks]*

Level 1: There is a brief description of either how the housefly picks up pathogens or how it spreads them to humans. *[1 to 2 marks]*

Level 2: There is some description of how the housefly picks up pathogens and how it spreads them to humans. *[3 to 4 marks]*

Level 3: There is a detailed description of how the housefly picks up pathogens and how it spreads them to humans. *[5 to 6 marks]*

Answers

Here are some points your answer may include:

Picking up pathogens:

The housefly uses its wings to fly to a dirty place, e.g. animal faeces, dustbin, rubbish dump, etc.

Pathogens stick to the fly's body.

Pathogens stick to the hairs on the fly's legs.

Pathogens are picked up on the fly's wings.

Pathogens are eaten by the fly.

Transfer to humans:

The fly uses its wings to travel to a human food source.

The fly secretes saliva on a human food source along with pathogens that the fly ate.

The housefly transfers pathogens onto a human food source from its body/leg hairs/wings.

The housefly deposits faeces onto a human food source.

Humans then eat the contaminated food source and take in the pathogens.

Pages 41-42 — Viral, Fungal and Protist Diseases

Warm-up

protist, vectors, fever, breeding

1.1 virus *[1 mark]*

1.2 The infected person coughs/sneezes *[1 mark]*.
The virus is carried in the air in droplets *[1 mark]*.
Other people on the train breathe in/inhale the droplets *[1 mark]*.

Remember, pathogens can be spread by water, through the air, by vectors, or by direct contact.

1.3 The person can be vaccinated against the pathogen *[1 mark]*.

2.1 antiretroviral drugs *[1 mark]*

2.2 the immune system *[1 mark]*

2.3 sexual contact *[1 mark]*, exchange of blood when people share needles *[1 mark]*

3.1 E.g. tomato plant *[1 mark]*.

3.2 The leaves have a mosaic pattern (where parts of the leaves become discoloured) *[1 mark]*.

3.3 The discolouration of the leaves means that the plant can't carry out photosynthesis as well, so growth is affected *[1 mark]*.

3.4 E.g. the diameter of the fruit from the infected plant is smaller than the healthy plant *[1 mark]*. The fruit from the infected plant has a lower/smaller mass than the healthy plant *[1 mark]*.

4.1 Purple or black spots develop on the leaves *[1 mark]*. These leaves can then turn yellow *[1 mark]* and drop off *[1 mark]*.

4.2 Because the disease can spread to other plants in water or by the wind *[1 mark]*.

4.3 If any leaves are left, the fungus could spread to other living rose plants *[1 mark]*.

By destroying the fungus, there won't be any left to spread to other plants.

Page 43 — Bacterial Diseases and Preventing Disease

1.1 Any two from: e.g. fever / stomach cramps / vomiting / diarrhoea *[2 marks]*.

1.2 toxins *[1 mark]*

1.3 The vaccination prevents the spread of the disease in poultry *[1 mark]*. This means that the poultry that humans eat won't be contaminated with the *Salmonella* bacteria *[1 mark]*.

1.4 E.g. by washing hands thoroughly after using the toilet. / By avoiding preparing food. / By the infected person being isolated from other individuals *[1 mark]*.

There's more than one right answer here — just think of any sensible way of preventing the bacteria from being transferred from person to person.

2.1 Through sexual contact *[1 mark]*.

2.2 E.g. pain when urinating *[1 mark]*. A thick yellow or green discharge from the vagina *[1 mark]*.

2.3 penicillin *[1 mark]*

2.4 condoms *[1 mark]*

Page 44 — Fighting Disease

1.1 It acts as a barrier to stop pathogens getting inside the body *[1 mark]*. It secretes antimicrobial substances, which kill pathogens *[1 mark]*.

1.2 It has hairs and mucus, which trap particles that could contain pathogens *[1 mark]*.

2 How to grade your answer:

Level 0: There is no relevant information. *[No marks]*

Level 1: There is a brief description of either the body's defences or the role of the immune system. *[1 to 2 marks]*

Level 2: There is at least one correct description of the body's defences and at least one correct description of the role of the immune system. *[3 to 4 marks]*

Level 3: There is more than one correct description of the body's defences and more than one correct description of the role of the immune system. *[5 to 6 marks]*

Here are some points your answer may include:

The body's defences:

The trachea and bronchi secrete mucus to trap pathogens that have entered the body.

The trachea and bronchi are lined with cilia.

Cilia are hair-like structures which waft mucus up to the back of the throat where it can be swallowed.

The stomach produces hydrochloric acid, which kills pathogens that have been swallowed.

The role of the immune system:

The immune system contains white blood cells, which travel round the body in the blood.

White blood cells can engulf pathogens and digest them — this is called phagocytosis.

White blood cells can produce antibodies that can kill pathogens.

White blood cells can produce antitoxins that counteract toxins produced by invading bacteria.

You wouldn't get marks for talking about the skin or about the hairs in the nose — they're there to stop pathogens getting inside your body in the first place. This question is asking you to describe that defences that the body has for pathogens that have managed to make it inside your body.

Answers

Page 45 — Fighting Disease — Vaccination

1.1   small amounts of dead/inactive pathogens *[1 mark]*

1.2   White blood cells are stimulated to produce antibodies *[1 mark]*.

2.1   Because the body would be able to rapidly mass-produce antibodies to kill off the mumps pathogens *[1 mark]*.

2.2   The large proportion of the population who have been vaccinated against the pathogen won't catch the disease *[1 mark]*. This means that the people who aren't vaccinated are unlikely to catch the disease because there are fewer people able to pass it on *[1 mark]*.

3.1   It would prevent the traveller from catching cholera whilst they are visiting the country *[1 mark]* and then bringing it back to their own country *[1 mark]*.

3.2   It prevents anyone from bringing certain diseases into the country *[1 mark]*.

Page 46 — Fighting Disease — Drugs

1.1   Viruses reproduce using your body cells *[1 mark]*, which makes it very difficult to develop drugs that destroy just the virus without killing the body's cells *[1 mark]*.

1.2   E.g. painkiller / cold remedy *[1 mark]*.

1.3   Because the drug is unable to kill pathogens *[1 mark]*.

2.1   Bacteria that can't be killed by an antibiotic *[1 mark]*.

2.2   The number of antibiotic-resistant infections increased between 2013 and 2015 *[1 mark]*.

2.3   153 − 84 = 69
(69 ÷ 84) × 100 = 82.14 = **82%** *[2 marks for correct answer, otherwise 1 mark for correct working]*

Page 47 — Developing Drugs

1.1   E.g. toxicity, efficacy and dosage *[3 marks]*

1.2   cells, tissues and live animals *[1 mark]*

It'd be no use testing on dead animals, as their cells and tissues won't respond in the same way as living tissues. You also wouldn't want to test on humans or patients at this stage, just in case the drug proves to be dangerous.

2.1   In case the drug has any harmful effects *[1 mark]*.

2.2   In double blind trials, patients would be randomly split into two groups *[1 mark]*. One group would be given a placebo and the other group would be given the drug *[1 mark]*. Neither the patients or the doctors would know who was in which group until after the results had been gathered *[1 mark]*.

2.3   It allows for the placebo effect. / It prevents the patient expecting the treatment to work and therefore feeling better, even though the treatment isn't doing anything. / It prevents the doctors who are analysing the results from being subconsciously influenced by their knowledge. *[1 mark]*

2.4   E.g. it helps to check that the work is valid. / It helps to prevent false claims *[1 mark]*.

2.5   E.g. to prevent them showing bias *[1 mark]* in their analysis of the results, and giving support to the results when in fact they weren't valid *[1 mark]*.

Pages 48-49 — Monoclonal Antibodies

Warm-up
     lymphocytes, fluorescent dye, attach to

1.1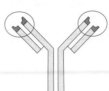

[1 mark]

1.2   Antigen A *[1 mark]*

2   Monoclonal antibodies are antibodies produced from lots of clones of a single white blood cell *[1 mark]*. This means all the antibodies are identical and will only target one specific protein antigen *[1 mark]*.

3.1   An anti-cancer drug/a radioactive substance/a toxic drug/ a chemical that stops cancer cells growing and dividing *[1 mark]* is attached to the monoclonal antibodies *[1 mark]*. The monoclonal antibodies target the cancer cells *[1 mark]* and deliver the substance without killing any normal body cells near the tumour *[1 mark]*.

3.2   They cause more side effects than were originally expected *[1 mark]*.

3.3   Any two from: e.g. in pregnancy tests. / Measuring the levels of hormones/chemicals in the blood. / Detecting pathogens. / Locating specific molecules on a cell/in a tissue *[2 marks]*.

4   How to grade your answer:
Level 0:   There is no relevant information.
[No marks]
Level 1:   There is a brief description of how monoclonal antibodies are made, but many details are missing. *[1 to 2 marks]*
Level 2:   There is some description of how monoclonal antibodies are made, but details are missing. *[3 to 4 marks]*
Level 3:   There is a clear and detailed description of how monoclonal antibodies are made.
[5 to 6 marks]

Here are some points your answer may include:
A mouse is injected with a specific antigen to make specific antibodies.
Lymphocytes are taken from the mouse.
A lymphocyte is fused with a tumour cell.
This creates a cell called a hybridoma.
The hybridoma cell can be cloned to get lots of identical cells.
These identical hybridoma cells produce monoclonal antibodies.
These antibodies can be collected and purified.

Pages 50-53 — Plant Diseases and Defences

1.1   E.g. tobacco mosaic virus *[1 mark]*.

1.2   E.g. (rose) black spot *[1 mark]*.

1.3   E.g. aphids *[1 mark]*.

2.1   Any four from: e.g. stunted growth / patches of decay/ rot / abnormal growths / malformed stems or leaves / discolouration *[4 marks]*.

2.2 Taking the plant to a laboratory where scientists can identify the pathogen *[1 mark]*. Using a testing kit that identifies the pathogen using monoclonal antibodies *[1 mark]*.

2.3 (6 ÷ 42) × 100 = 14.29 = **14%** *[2 marks for correct answer, otherwise 1 mark for correct working]*

3.1 They provide a physical barrier against pathogens to stop them from entering cells *[1 mark]*.

3.2 Antibacterial chemicals *[1 mark]* kill bacterial pathogens that could damage the plants *[1 mark]*. Poisons *[1 mark]* deter herbivores from eating the plants *[1 mark]*.

3.3 Any two from: e.g. thorns or hairs on its surface — these stop animals from touching and eating the plant. / Leaves that droop or curl when something touches them — this means that plants can knock insects off themselves and move away from things that might eat them. / Mimicry of other organisms — this tricks other organisms into not eating or laying eggs on the plant *[1 mark for each correct adaptation and 1 mark for each correct explanation linked to an adaptation, up to 4 marks]*.

4.1 E.g. nitrates *[1 mark]*.

4.2 E.g. nitrates are needed to make proteins *[1 mark]*, which plants need to grow *[1 mark]*.

4.3 E.g. magnesium ions *[1 mark]*.

4.4 E.g. the plant will have a lack of chlorophyll/suffer from chlorosis *[1 mark]* and will have yellow leaves *[1 mark]*.

5.1 The plants with a complete mineral supply had a dry mass of 8.5 g *[1 mark]*. The magnesium-deficient plants and the nitrate-deficient plants both had a dry mass of 4 g *[1 mark]*, which is about half the mass of the plants with a complete mineral supply *[1 mark]*.

The question tells you to use data from the graph in your answer, so make sure that you do, or you'll lose marks. You'd also get the last mark here if you wrote the statement the other way round (if you said that the plants with a complete mineral supply had about twice the dry mass of the other plants).

5.2 The dependent variable is the dry mass of the plants *[1 mark]*. The independent variable is the mineral content of the growth medium *[1 mark]*.

5.3 E.g. plant some seedlings in a complete growth medium and the same number in a growth medium deficient in phosphate *[1 mark]*. Grow the plants in the same conditions for 20 days *[1 mark]*. Record the length of all the leaves on each seedling and calculate an average length for each group *[1 mark]*.

You don't have to describe exactly this experiment to get the marks here. It's just 1 mark for putting some plants in a phosphate-deficient medium and some in a normal medium, 1 mark for growing them for a bit under the same conditions, and 1 mark for some way of comparing their leaf size at the end.

6.1 To kill any pathogens that might be on the skewer, so the scientist knows that any pathogens she transfers come from the pear *[1 mark]*.

6.2 The hole that doesn't have any material added to it is a control. / To show that it must be the pathogen, and not making the hole, that causes any symptoms that develop *[1 mark]*.

6.3 There will be a soft, brown patch around the hole that was infected with material from the unhealthy pear *[1 mark]*. The hole on the other side of the pear won't have a soft, brown patch *[1 mark]*.

6.4 E.g. get someone else to repeat her experiment and show that they get similar results *[1 mark]*.

Topic 4 — Bioenergetics

Page 54 — Photosynthesis and Limiting Factors

1.1 the Sun / the environment *[1 mark]*

1.2 **carbon dioxide** *[1 mark]* + water → glucose + **oxygen** *[1 mark]*

1.3 cellulose *[1 mark]*

1.4 Any two from: e.g. for respiration. / For making amino acids (which are used to make proteins) by combining the glucose with nitrate ions. / It is converted to lipids (fats and oils) for storage. / It is turned into starch for storage *[2 marks]*.

2.1 An endothermic reaction is where energy is transferred from the environment during the process *[1 mark]*.

2.2 nitrate concentration *[1 mark]*

2.3 The rate of photosynthesis would decrease *[1 mark]* because the chloroplasts wouldn't be able to absorb as much light *[1 mark]*.

Pages 55-57 — The Rate of Photosynthesis

Warm-up

low, slowly, high, damaged

1.1 Any two from: e.g. adding a heater — to increase the temperature, which will increase the rate of photosynthesis. / Supplying artificial light — to increase the light intensity, which will increase the rate of photosynthesis. / Adding a paraffin heater — to increase the carbon dioxide concentration, which will increase the rate of photosynthesis. *[1 mark for each correct improvement and 1 mark for each correct explanation, up to 4 marks]*.

1.2 Because the farmer will get a better yield *[1 mark]*, which means they will also make more money/profit *[1 mark]*.

2.1 At first, as the carbon dioxide concentration increases, the rate of photosynthesis increases as well *[1 mark]*. Then, at 0.10 arbitrary units of carbon dioxide, the graph flattens out — as the carbon dioxide concentration increases, the rate of photosynthesis no longer increases *[1 mark]*.

2.2 E.g. temperature *[1 mark]*, light intensity *[1 mark]*.

2.3

[1 mark for correctly labelled axes, 1 mark for correctly sketched line]

Answers

3.1 It will increase *[1 mark]*.

3.2 distance = 20 cm, so 20^2 = 400 *[1 mark]*
1 ÷ 400 = **0.0025 arbitrary units** *[1 mark]*

3.3 How to grade your answer:
Level 0: There is no relevant information. *[No marks]*
Level 1: There is a brief description of a method used to investigate the effect of temperature on the rate of photosynthesis, with no control variables mentioned. *[1 to 2 marks]*
Level 2: There is some description of a method used to investigate the effect of temperature on the rate of photosynthesis, including an example of a variable to control. *[3 to 4 marks]*
Level 3: There is detailed description of a method used to investigate the effect of temperature on the rate of photosynthesis, including more than one example of variables to control. *[5 to 6 marks]*

Here are some points your answer may include:
A test tube is clamped in place in a water bath at a particular temperature, e.g. 10 °C.
Once the water in the test tube has reached the correct temperature, the pondweed is added to the test tube and the test tube is sealed.
A capillary tube and syringe are attached to the test tube. The pondweed is left to photosynthesise for a set amount of time.
At the end of the experiment, the syringe is used to draw the gas bubble in the capillary tube up alongside a ruler and the length of the gas bubble that has formed is measured. This is proportional to the volume of oxygen produced.
The experiment is repeated twice at this starting temperature.
Then the whole experiment is repeated at different temperatures, e.g. 15 °C, 20 °C, 25 °C.
The variables that should be controlled in this experiment include light intensity and the concentration of carbon dioxide.

Pages 58-59 — Respiration and Metabolism

1.1 exothermic (reaction) *[1 mark]*

1.2 E.g. to build up larger molecules from smaller ones *[1 mark]*.
To allow the gull's muscles to contract *[1 mark]*.
To keep the gull's body temperature steady in cooler surroundings *[1 mark]*.

2.1 Plants, e.g: cellulose / starch / proteins *[1 mark]*
Animals, e.g: glycogen / proteins *[1 mark]*

2.2 A lipid is made from one molecule of glycerol *[1 mark]* and three fatty acids *[1 mark]*.

2.3 Glucose is combined with nitrate ions *[1 mark]* to make amino acids, which are then made into proteins *[1 mark]*.

2.4 urea *[1 mark]*

3.1 Any two from: e.g. the mass of the peas or glass beads in the flask / the size of the flask / the type of peas / the temperature outside of the flasks / the temperature of the peas at the start of the experiment *[2 marks]*.

3.2 E.g. she could repeat her experiment and calculate a mean temperature increase for each flask *[1 mark]*.

3.3 The boiled peas will not germinate, so flask 2 is included to show that the increase in temperature in flask 1 is due to the peas germinating *[1 mark]*. Flask 3 is included to show that the temperature change is due to the presence of the peas and no other factor *[1 mark]*.

The temperature in flask 3 should remain constant — if it changed, this would suggest there was an error in the experiment.

3.4 E.g. she could include another flask that contained disinfected boiled peas. / She could disinfect the peas (and the glass beads) with an antiseptic before starting the experiment *[1 mark]*.

If there was no temperature change in a flask containing disinfected boiled peas, the student could conclude that the temperature increase in the flask of boiled peas in her first experiment was due to the presence of microorganisms.

Pages 60-61 — Aerobic and Anaerobic Respiration

Warm-up
Aerobic respiration — Respiration using oxygen.
Anaerobic respiration — Respiration without oxygen.
Fermentation — Respiration without oxygen.

1.1 E.g. the snail must have enough oxygen for two hours / the snail must not dry out *[1 mark]*.

1.2 The percentage of carbon dioxide in the air has increased over the two hours because the snail gives out carbon dioxide as it respires *[1 mark]*.

1.3 The percentage of carbon dioxide in the air has stayed the same over the two hours because the glass beads were not respiring *[1 mark]*.

1.4 It will have decreased *[1 mark]* because the snail will have used up oxygen as it respired *[1 mark]*.

1.5 To show that it's the snail producing carbon dioxide (and not just the presence of something in the beaker) *[1 mark]*.

2.1 glucose *[1 mark]*

2.2 Ethanol — to make alcoholic drinks *[1 mark]*.
Carbon dioxide — to make bread rise *[1 mark]*.

3 Aerobic respiration in muscle cells uses oxygen, whereas anaerobic respiration doesn't *[1 mark]*. Aerobic respiration in muscle cells forms carbon dioxide and water, whereas anaerobic respiration forms lactic acid *[1 mark]*. Aerobic respiration in muscles cells transfers a lot of energy, whereas anaerobic respiration in muscle cells transfers a small amount of energy *[1 mark]*.

Pages 62-63 — Exercise

Warm-up
muscles, oxygen debt, oxygen, lactic acid

1.1 (12 + 11 + 12) ÷ 3 = 11.6... = **12** breaths per minute *[1 mark]*

1.2 During exercise the breathing rate increased *[1 mark]* to get more oxygen into the blood *[1 mark]*, which was needed for increased respiration in the muscles *[1 mark]*.

Answers

1.3 The breathing rate remained high one minute after exercise *[1 mark]* because there were still high levels of lactic acid and carbon dioxide in the blood *[1 mark]*. The high breathing rate helps remove these from the body *[1 mark]*. The breathing rate had returned to normal by five minutes after exercise *[1 mark]* because the oxygen debt had been paid off *[1 mark]*.

1.4 breath volume *[1 mark]*, heart rate *[1 mark]*

2.1 80 – 20 = 60
(60 ÷ 20) × 100 = **300%** *[2 marks for correct answer, otherwise 1 mark for correct working.]*

2.2 The muscles started to respire anaerobically *[1 mark]*, which formed lactic acid *[1 mark]* as a result of the incomplete oxidation of glucose *[1 mark]*.

2.3 They become fatigued *[1 mark]* and stop contracting efficiently *[1 mark]*.

2.4 Blood transports the lactic acid to the liver *[1 mark]*, where it is converted back to glucose *[1 mark]*.

Topic 5 — Homeostasis and Response

Page 64 — Homeostasis

1.1 The regulation of the conditions inside the body/cells to maintain a stable internal environment *[1 mark]* in response to changes in internal and external conditions *[1 mark]*.

1.2 They maintain the right conditions for cells to function properly. / They maintain the right conditions for enzyme action *[1 mark]*.

1.3 receptor *[1 mark]*

1.4 The receptors detect that the blood pressure is too high and send a signal to the coordination centre *[1 mark]*. The coordination centre processes the information and organises a response / stimulates an effector *[1 mark]*. The effector produces a response to decrease the blood pressure (back to its optimum level) *[1 mark]*.

You don't need to know all about the regulation of blood pressure to answer this question — you just need to know the sequence of events in a negative feedback response, from receptors to effectors.

2.1 15 minutes *[1 mark]*

2.2 30 – 20 = 10 min
35.0 – 34.5 = 0.5 °C
0.5 ÷ 10 = **0.05 °C/min** *[2 marks for correct answer, otherwise 1 mark for correct working.]*

Pages 65-66 — The Nervous System

1.1 X — brain *[1 mark]*
Y— spinal cord *[1 mark]*

1.2 central nervous system/CNS *[1 mark]*

1.3 It receives information from receptors and coordinates a response (which is carried out by effectors) *[1 mark]*.

2.1 It allows organisms to react to their surroundings *[1 mark]* and coordinate their behaviour *[1 mark]*.

2.2 Spinal cord — coordinator *[1 mark]*
Bright light — stimulus *[1 mark]*
Blinking — response *[1 mark]*

2.3 Sensory neurones *[1 mark]* and motor neurones *[1 mark]*.

2.4 Muscles — contract *[1 mark]*
Glands — secrete hormones *[1 mark]*

3.1 E.g. it will reduce the effect of random errors on their results *[1 mark]*.

3.2 uncertainty = range ÷ 2 = (25 – 15) ÷ 2 = 10 ÷ 2
= **± 5 mm** *[2 marks for correct answer, otherwise 1 mark for correct working.]*

3.3 E.g. move the toothpicks together at smaller intervals (e.g. 1 mm) around the point where the person can only feel one toothpick *[1 mark]*.

3.4 Repeat the experiment on the forearm more times to see if it still doesn't fit in with the rest of the results *[1 mark]*.

3.5 The students have only tested three parts of the body / they haven't tested all parts of the body *[1 mark]*, so they can only conclude that the palm is the most sensitive out of the parts tested *[1 mark]*.

Page 67 — Synapses and Reflexes

Warm-up
Dropping a hot plate. The pupil widening in dim light.

1 Reflex reactions are rapid and automatic. *[1 mark]*

2.1 X — sensory neurone *[1 mark]*
Y — relay neurone *[1 mark]*
Z — motor neurone *[1 mark]*

2.2 stimulus — flame/fire *[1 mark]*
coordinator — spinal cord / relay neurone *[1 mark]*
effector — muscle *[1 mark]*

2.3 synapse *[1 mark]*

2.4 Chemicals diffuse across the gap and transfer the nerve signal *[1 mark]*.

Page 68 — Investigating Reaction Time

1.1 Student 2 = (0.16 + 0.13 + 0.15) ÷ 3 = 0.1466...
= **0.15 s** *[1 mark]*
Student 3 = (0.20 + 0.22 + 0.19) ÷ 3 = 0.2033...
= **0.20 s** *[1 mark]*

1.2 Student 1, Test 3 (0.43 s) *[1 mark]*

1.3 The students' reaction times without caffeine would act as a control for each student *[1 mark]*. The results from each student's tests could then be compared to the control to see if caffeine actually had an effect on reaction time *[1 mark]*.

1.4 E.g. the reaction times of student 1, 2 and 3 will be affected to different extents by caffeine due to natural variation between them *[1 mark]*, so the investigation isn't a fair test *[1 mark]*. / Two variables (the caffeinated drink and the student) are being changed *[1 mark]*, so the investigation isn't a fair test *[1 mark]*.

1.5 Any three from: e.g. the hand that the student used to catch the ruler. / The height from which the ruler was dropped. / The ruler used. / The person dropping the ruler. / The way that the student was positioned to catch the ruler. / The time between the consumption of caffeine and the test.
[3 marks — 1 mark for each correct answer.]

You wouldn't get a mark for saying that the amount of caffeine given to each student should be the same each time, because this was said in the question.

Answers

Page 69 — The Brain

1.1   neurones *[1 mark]*

1.2   medulla *[1 mark]*

1.3   E.g. breathing, heart beat *[2 marks]*.

2.1   A *[1 mark]*

2.2   B *[1 mark]*

2.3   The brain is very complex *[1 mark]*.
      The brain is very delicate *[1 mark]*.

2.4   Electrically stimulating different parts of the brain *[1 mark]*. Studying patients with brain damage *[1 mark]*.

Pages 70-71 — The Eye

Warm-up

     Clockwise from top left: iris, retina, sclera, optic nerve, lens, pupil.

1.1   retina *[1 mark]*

1.2   brain *[1 mark]*

1.3   cornea *[1 mark]*

1.4   iris *[1 mark]*

1.5   Ciliary muscles *[1 mark]* and suspensory ligaments *[1 mark]*.

2.1   The pupil of eye B is bigger/wider than eye A *[1 mark]* and the iris is smaller/thinner *[1 mark]*.

2.2   Eye B, because the pupil is wider to let in more light *[1 mark]*.

2.3   So that the amount of light entering the eye can be controlled *[1 mark]* so that bright light cannot damage the retina / to allow sufficient light to enter the eye in dim conditions *[1 mark]*.

3   Level 0:   There is no relevant information. *[No marks]*

           Level 1:   There is a brief description of how accommodation works for either near vision or distant vision. *[1 to 2 marks]*

           Level 2:   There is some description of how accommodation works for both near and distant vision. *[3 to 4 marks]*

           Level 3:   There is a detailed description of how accommodation works for both near and distant vision. *[5 to 6 marks]*

     Here are some points your answer may include:
Accommodation is the process of focusing light on the retina by changing the shape of the lens.
To focus on a near object:

- the ciliary muscles contract,
- the suspensory ligaments slacken,
- the lens becomes fat / more curved,
- the lens refracts light rays strongly.

To focus on a distant object:

- the ciliary muscles relax,
- the suspensory ligaments are pulled tight,
- the lens is then pulled thin / becomes less curved,
- the lens only refracts light rays slightly.

Page 72 — Correcting Vision Defects

1.1   short-sightedness / myopia *[1 mark]*

1.2   The spectacle lens refracts/bends light rays *[1 mark]* so that they focus on the retina *[1 mark]*.

1.3   behind the retina *[1 mark]*

1.4   convex lens *[1 mark]*

2.1   It changes the shape of the cornea *[1 mark]* to change how strongly light is refracted into the eye *[1 mark]*.

2.2   replacement lens surgery *[1 mark]*

2.3   E.g. the retina could be damaged. / The eye may become infected. *[1 mark]*

2.4   contact lenses *[1 mark]*

Pages 73-74 — Controlling Body Temperature

1.1   brain *[1 mark]*

1.2   temperature of the blood *[1 mark]*

1.3   The skin contains temperature receptors *[1 mark]*. These send nervous impulses to the thermoregulatory centre *[1 mark]*.

2.1   When the body temperature becomes too high, energy is transferred from the blood and skin to the environment *[1 mark]*. The blood vessels dilate so more blood can flow near the surface of the skin *[1 mark]* and sweat evaporates from the skin *[1 mark]*.

2.2   When the body temperature becomes too low, the transfer of energy from the blood and skin to the environment is reduced *[1 mark]* by vasoconstriction (and lack of sweating) *[1 mark]*. The body also shivers, which uses respiration to transfer energy to the body (from glucose) *[1 mark]*.

3.1

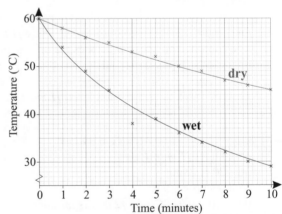

[2 marks for all eleven points plotted correctly, otherwise 1 mark for any eight points plotted correctly. 1 mark for a smooth curve of best fit that ignores the anomalous result.]

3.2   E.g. over ten minutes, the temperature of the water in the boiling tube with the wet paper towel decreased more than the temperature of the water in the boiling tube with the dry paper towel. / The water temperature decreased more rapidly in the boiling tube with the wet paper towel than in the boiling tube with the dry paper towel *[1 mark]*.

Answers

3.3 Any two from, e.g. the volume of water in each boiling tube / the length/volume of paper wrapped around each tube / the air temperature surrounding the boiling tubes / the initial temperature of the water in each boiling tube *[2 marks]*.

3.4 The wet paper towel represents sweat on the skin *[1 mark]*. Evaporation of water from the paper works in the same way as evaporation of sweat from the skin *[1 mark]*. The dry tube acts as a control/shows that the evaporation from the wet towel cools the tube faster *[1 mark]*.

Page 75 — The Endocrine System

1.1 Glands secrete hormones directly into the blood. *[1 mark]*

1.2 Hormones are chemical molecules. *[1 mark]*

1.3 E.g. the effects of the endocrine system are slower *[1 mark]*. The effects of the endocrine system are longer lasting *[1 mark]*.

2.1 A — pituitary gland *[1 mark]*
B — thyroid *[1 mark]*
C — adrenal gland *[1 mark]*
D — pancreas *[1 mark]*
E — ovary *[1 mark]*

2.2 pituitary gland *[1 mark]*

2.3 They act on other glands *[1 mark]* to direct them to release other hormones that bring about change *[1 mark]*.

Pages 76-77 — Controlling Blood Glucose

1.1 pancreas *[1 mark]*

1.2 insulin *[1 mark]*

1.3 It moves into liver and muscle cells *[1 mark]* and is converted to glycogen for storage *[1 mark]*.

2.1 The pancreas produces little or no insulin *[1 mark]*.

2.2 Uncontrolled high blood glucose level *[1 mark]*.

2.3 E.g. the person's diet. / How active the person is. *[1 mark]*

2.4 The body cells no longer respond to the insulin produced by the pancreas *[1 mark]*.

2.5 Eat a carbohydrate-controlled diet *[1 mark]* and get regular exercise *[1 mark]*.

2.6 being overweight / obesity *[1 mark]*

3.1 The blood glucose concentration starts increasing as glucose from the drink is absorbed into the blood *[1 mark]*. The pancreas detects a high blood glucose concentration and secretes insulin *[1 mark]*. Insulin causes the blood glucose concentration to fall back down *[1 mark]*.

3.2 glucagon *[1 mark]*

3.3 It increases the concentration of glucose in the blood *[1 mark]*.

3.4 Glucagon causes glycogen to be converted into glucose and be released into the blood *[1 mark]*.

3.5 E.g. after drinking the glucose drink, the blood glucose concentration would carry on increasing / stay high / not start to fall / fall more slowly *[1 mark]*.

Pages 78-79 — The Kidneys

Warm-up

blood, cells, osmosis, ions, kidneys

1.1 filtration *[1 mark]*

1.2 urea *[1 mark]*

1.3 selective reabsorption *[1 mark]*

1.4 Any two from: glucose / water / ions *[2 marks]*.

2.1 From the lungs when breathing out *[1 mark]*.

2.2 ions *[1 mark]* / urea *[1 mark]*

2.3 The body can't control water loss from the skin. *[1 mark]*

3.1 liver *[1 mark]*

3.2 protein in the diet *[1 mark]*

3.3 ammonia *[1 mark]*

3.4 It is toxic *[1 mark]*.

4 How to grade your answer:
Level 0: There is no relevant information. *[No marks]*
Level 1: There are some relevant points describing the body's response to low water content but the answer is missing some detail. *[1 to 2 marks]*
Level 2: There is a clear, detailed description of the body's response to low water content that includes the hormone and structures involved. *[3 to 4 marks]*

Here are some points your answer may include:
A signal is sent to the pituitary gland to release more ADH (anti-diuretic hormone).
ADH causes the kidneys/kidney tubules to reabsorb more water.
This means less water is lost in the urine.
So the water content of the blood is increased.

Page 80 — Kidney Failure

1.1 Because their kidneys don't work properly to control the levels of dissolved substances in their body (and remove waste products) *[1 mark]*.

1.2 urea / excess ions / excess water *[1 mark]*

1.3 Proteins are too large pass through the partially permeable membrane *[1 mark]*.

1.4 So that useful substances won't be lost from the person's blood during dialysis *[1 mark]*.

1.5 Any two from: glucose / water / ions *[2 marks]*.

2 Advantage — e.g. the person can lead a normal life after the transplant. / The patient doesn't need to spend hours on dialysis any more. *[1 mark]*
Disadvantage — e.g. waiting lists are long. / It is not always easy to find a donor. / The donor organ could be rejected by the patient's immune system. *[1 mark]*

Page 81 — Puberty and the Menstrual Cycle

1.1 oestrogen *[1 mark]*

1.2 ovulation *[1 mark]*

1.3 Every 28 days *[1 mark]*.

1.4 luteinising hormone *[1 mark]*

162

Answers

1.5 testosterone *[1 mark]*
1.6 testes *[1 mark]*
2.1 oestrogen *[1 mark]*, progesterone *[1 mark]*
2.2 pituitary gland *[1 mark]*
2.3 It causes an egg to mature in one of the ovaries *[1 mark]* and stimulates the ovaries to produce hormones/oestrogen *[1 mark]*.
2.4 oestrogen *[1 mark]*

Pages 82-83 — Controlling Fertility

Warm-up

Hormonal	Non-hormonal
contraceptive injection plastic intrauterine device contraceptive patch	abstinence condom diaphragm sterilisation

1.1 As a tablet taken by mouth. *[1 mark]*
1.2 The hormones inhibit FSH production *[1 mark]*.
1.3 progesterone *[1 mark]*
1.4 It stops the maturation/release of eggs. / It makes it hard for sperm to swim to the egg. / It stops any fertilised egg implanting in the uterus. *[1 mark]*
2.1 condom *[1 mark]*
2.2 female condom / diaphragm *[1 mark]*
2.3 They prevent the sperm reaching an egg *[1 mark]*.
2.4 spermicidal agents / spermicides *[1 mark]*
2.5 Avoiding intercourse when the woman is at the most fertile point in her menstrual cycle *[1 mark]*.
2.6 sterilisation *[1 mark]*
2.7 condom *[1 mark]*
3.1 E.g. the woman does not have to remember to take the contraceptive every day *[1 mark]*.
3.2 E.g. the injection lasts for several months, so if she has any side effects they may last for a long time *[1 mark]*.
3.3 E.g. barrier methods do not have the possible side effects associated with taking hormones *[1 mark]*.

Page 84 — More on Controlling Fertility

1.1 FSH is needed to stimulate eggs to mature. / No eggs would be released so the woman would not be able to become pregnant. *[1 mark]*
1.2 Luteinising hormone / LH *[1 mark]* because it stimulates the release of an egg *[1 mark]*.
1.3 Advantage: e.g. the woman may become pregnant naturally / without needing IVF *[1 mark]*. Disadvantage: e.g. some women need several treatments so it can be expensive. / Too many eggs may be stimulated resulting in unexpected multiple pregnancies. *[1 mark]*
2.1 The mother is given FSH and LH *[1 mark]* to stimulate the maturation of several eggs *[1 mark]*. Several eggs are collected from the mother and fertilised by sperm from the father in a laboratory *[1 mark]*. The fertilised eggs are grown into embryos in the laboratory *[1 mark]*. At the stage when they are tiny balls of cells, one or two embryos are inserted into the mother's uterus *[1 mark]*.

2.2 Any two from: e.g. the treatment may not work so repeated attempts are needed, which could be upsetting/stressful for the couple. / It can result in multiple births which can be a risk to the mother's health. / The mother may have a strong reaction to the hormones (e.g. pain, vomiting). *[2 marks]*

Page 85 — Adrenaline and Thyroxine

Warm-up
Clockwise from top left: high, inhibited, normal, stimulated, low.
1.1 Thyroxine regulates basal metabolic rate *[1 mark]*.
1.2 thyroid gland *[1 mark]*
2.1 adrenal glands *[1 mark]*
2.2 E.g. it increases heart rate *[1 mark]*, which boosts the delivery of oxygen to the brain and muscles *[1 mark]* and also boosts the delivery of glucose to the brain and muscles *[1 mark]*.
2.3 flight or fight *[1 mark]*

Pages 86-87 — Plant Hormones

1.1 The seedlings in Set A have grown straight up but the seedlings in Set B have grown sideways (towards the light) *[1 mark]*.
1.2 phototropism *[1 mark]*
1.3 It allows the plant to receive maximum light for photosynthesis *[1 mark]*.
1.4 Auxin moved towards the shaded side of the shoot / away from the light side of the shoot *[1 mark]*. The auxin made the cells elongate/grow faster on the shaded side *[1 mark]*. So the shoot bent towards the light *[1 mark]*.
2.1 positive gravitropism/geotropism *[1 mark]*
2.2 shoot *[1 mark]*
2.3 downwards / away from light *[1 mark]*
3.1 E.g. Group C shows that blocking the diffusion of substances from the tip to the rest of the shoot prevents growth *[1 mark]*.
3.2 Yes. Auxin is produced by the tips of shoots *[1 mark]*, so the results support the student's hypothesis because they show that shoots with the tips intact (Group A) and shoots with tips that were removed but then replaced above a permeable barrier (Group B) grew *[1 mark]*, and that shoots with tips that were removed (Group D) or removed then replaced above an impermeable barrier (Group C) did not grow *[1 mark]*.
3.3 E.g. set up a group of seedlings that have their tips cut off and place a piece of agar/sponge/paper that has been soaked in a solution of auxin on top of the cut shoots *[1 mark]*. Leave this group in the same conditions as before / leave to grow alongside a new Group A and Group D for a week, to see if the shoots grow *[1 mark]*.
By giving the cut shoots a source of auxin without replacing the tip, the student could see whether auxin is likely to be the missing factor that is preventing the shoots from growing (and not another substance in the tip).

Answers

Answers

Page 88 — Commercial Uses of Plant Hormones

1.1   ethene *[1 mark]*

1.2   seed germination *[1 mark]*

2   To end seed dormancy / cause seeds to germinate *[1 mark]*. To induce flowering *[1 mark]*. To grow larger fruit *[1 mark]*.

3.1   ethene *[1 mark]*

3.2   The fruit is firmer and so it is less easily damaged *[1 mark]*. It can then be ripened on the way to the supermarket so that it's perfect when it reaches the shelves *[1 mark]*.

4.1   auxin *[1 mark]*

4.2   To stimulate the cutting to develop roots *[1 mark]*.

4.3   selective weedkiller *[1 mark]*

Topic 6 — Inheritance, Variation and Evolution

Page 89 — DNA

1.1   DNA is located in the nucleus of animal and plant cells *[1 mark]*.

1.2   The structures that contain DNA *[1 mark]*.

2.1   Genes code for particular sequences of amino acids *[1 mark]*, which are put together to make specific proteins *[1 mark]*.

2.2   The entire set of genetic material in an organism *[1 mark]*.

2.3   E.g. it allows scientists to identify genes that are linked to different types of diseases *[1 mark]*. Knowing which genes are linked to inherited diseases could help us to develop effective treatments for them *[1 mark]*.

Pages 90-91 — The Structure of DNA and Protein Synthesis

1.1   A, C, G and T *[1 mark]*

1.2   A = phosphate *[1 mark]*, B = sugar *[1 mark]*

1.3

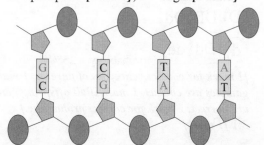

[1 mark for correct labelling of both C bases, 1 mark for correct labelling of both T bases. Maximum of 2 marks available.]

1.4   Each sequence of three bases codes for one specific amino acid *[1 mark]*, so the order of the bases in the gene decides the order of the amino acids in the chain *[1 mark]*.

2.1   ribosomes *[1 mark]*

2.2   They switch specific genes on or off *[1 mark]*.

3.1   A molecule called mRNA is made by copying the code from the DNA *[1 mark]*. The mRNA carries the code from the DNA to the site of protein synthesis *[1 mark]*.

3.2   Carrier molecules *[1 mark]* bring the amino acids coded for by the messenger molecule/mRNA to the site of protein synthesis *[1 mark]* in the correct order *[1 mark]*.

3.3   It folds up into a unique shape *[1 mark]*, which allows the protein to perform the task it is meant to do *[1 mark]*.

3.4   E.g. hormones *[1 mark]*. These are used to carry messages around the body *[1 mark]*.
E.g. enzymes *[1 mark]*. These act as biological catalysts to speed up chemical reactions in the body *[1 mark]*.

Page 92 — Mutations

Warm-up

False, True, False

1.1   AAGCTTCCGA *[1 mark]*

1.2   Because mutations change the sequence of DNA bases in a gene *[1 mark]*, and it is this sequence that codes for the specific amino acids in a protein *[1 mark]*. A change in the amino acids coded for could lead to a change in the protein *[1 mark]*.

1.3   E.g. the mutation could cause the structural protein to lose its strength *[1 mark]*, meaning that it may no longer be able to carry out its job of providing structure and support *[1 mark]*.

1.4   E.g. the shape of the enzyme's active site could be changed *[1 mark]*, meaning that its substrate may no longer be able to bind to it *[1 mark]*, so the enzyme would no longer be able to catalyse the reaction *[1 mark]*.

Page 93 — Reproduction

1.1   sperm *[1 mark]*

1.2   egg (cell) *[1 mark]*

1.3   meiosis *[1 mark]*

1.4   clones *[1 mark]*

1.5   mitosis *[1 mark]*

2.1   Because gametes only have half the number of chromosomes of a normal cell *[1 mark]*, so when two gametes fuse together the fertilised egg cell has the full number of chromosomes *[1 mark]*.

2.2   Any four from: e.g. asexual reproduction only involves one parent, whereas sexual reproduction involves two. / Unlike in sexual reproduction, there is no fusion of gametes in asexual reproduction. / Unlike in sexual reproduction, there is no mixing of chromosomes in asexual reproduction. / Unlike sexual reproduction, asexual reproduction doesn't give rise to genetic variation (as the offspring are genetically identical to the parent). / Asexual reproduction doesn't involve meiosis, whereas sexual reproduction does.
[4 marks — 1 mark for each correct answer.]

Answers

Page 94 — Meiosis

1.1 In the reproductive organs / ovaries and testes *[1 mark]*.
1.2 It is duplicated *[1 mark]*.
1.3 two *[1 mark]*
1.4 Four gametes are produced *[1 mark]*, each with only a single set of chromosomes *[1 mark]*. Each of the gametes is genetically different from the others *[1 mark]*.
2.1 two *[1 mark]*
2.2 mitosis *[1 mark]*
2.3 They differentiate into different types of specialised cell *[1 mark]*.

Page 95 — More on Reproduction

Warm-up
runners, seeds, identical, different
1.1 asexual *[1 mark]*
1.2 Malaria parasites reproduce asexually in the human host, but sexually in the mosquito *[1 mark]*.
2.1 Any two from: e.g. asexual reproduction uses less energy than sexual reproduction because organisms don't have to find a mate. / Asexual reproduction is faster than sexual reproduction because organisms don't have to find a mate. / Many identical offspring can be produced in favourable conditions. *[2 marks — 1 mark for each correct answer.]*
2.2 Because it creates genetic variation in the offspring *[1 mark]*. Variation means it's likely that some individuals in the population will have a gene that makes them better adapted to survive in the new environment *[1 mark]*. Individuals with this gene are more likely to survive and breed successfully *[1 mark]* and pass the gene on to future generations, which will allow them to also survive in the environment *[1 mark]*.

Page 96 — X and Y Chromosomes

1.1 23 pairs of chromosomes *[1 mark]*
1.2

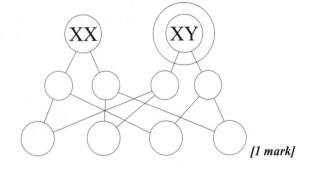

[1 mark]

1.3

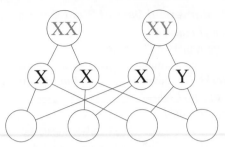

[1 mark for all gametes correct]

1.4

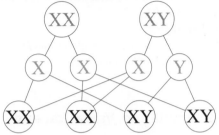

[1 mark if all the offspring genotypes are correct]

1.5 50:50 / 1:1 *[1 mark]*
1.6 E.g.

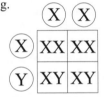

[1 mark for correct gametes of parents, 1 mark for correct genotypes of offspring.]

Pages 97-98 — Genetic Diagrams

Warm-up
alleles, recessive, homozygous, heterozygous, a single gene, multiple genes
1.1 Because there are carriers who don't have the disease *[1 mark]*.
1.2

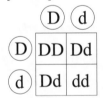

probability = **25%**
[1 mark for correct genotypes of parents, 1 mark if all gametes are correct, 1 mark if all offspring genotypes are correct, 1 mark for correct probability.]

2.1 3:1 *[1 mark]*
2.2

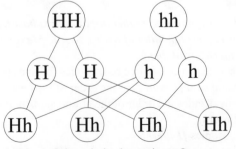

number of short-haired puppies = **8**
[1 mark for correct gametes, 1 mark for correct offspring genotypes, 1 mark for correct number of short-haired puppies.]

Answers

2.3 E.g.

ratio = **1:1**

[1 mark if all gametes are correct, 1 mark if all offspring genotypes are correct, 1 mark for correct probability.]

Page 99 — Inherited Disorders

1.1 Being born with extra fingers or toes *[1 mark]*.

1.2 That the allele for polydactyly is dominant *[1 mark]*.

1.3 Because the allele for cystic fibrosis is recessive *[1 mark]*, so the offspring must have two copies of the allele to have the disorder *[1 mark]*. There is only a 1 in 4 chance of this occurring when each parent has one copy of the allele *[1 mark]*.

2.1 E.g. it implies that people with genetic problems are undesirable, which could increase prejudice *[1 mark]*. Screening is expensive *[1 mark]*. There could become a point where everyone wants to screen their embryo in IVF to pick the most desirable one *[1 mark]*.

2.2 E.g. it will help to stop people suffering from genetic disorders *[1 mark]*. Treating disorders costs the government and taxpayer a lot of money. Screening to reduce the number of people with disorders could save money *[1 mark]*. Parents cannot use it to select desirable characteristics for their baby, as there are laws to stop screening going too far *[1 mark]*.

Page 100 — The Work of Mendel

Warm-up

genetics, mid-19th century, plants, passed on

1.1 Because the scientists of the day didn't have the background knowledge necessary to properly understand his findings. / Because the scientists of the day didn't know about genes, DNA and chromosomes. *[1 mark]*

1.2 In the late 1800s, scientists were able to observe how chromosomes behaved during cell division *[1 mark]*. Then in the early 20th century, scientists realised that there were striking similarities in the way that chromosomes and Mendel's 'hereditary units' acted *[1 mark]*. Based on this, it was proposed that the 'units' were found on chromosomes, and we now know these 'units' as genes *[1 mark]*. In the mid-20th century, the structure of DNA was determined *[1 mark]*. This allowed scientists to go on and find out exactly how genes work *[1 mark]*.

Page 101 — Variation

1.1 genetic *[1 mark]*

1.2 environmental *[1 mark]*

2 The mutation could lead to a new phenotype *[1 mark]*. If the environment changes, the new phenotype could make the individual more suited to the new environment *[1 mark]*. It could then become common throughout the species relatively quickly by natural selection *[1 mark]*.

Pages 102-103 — Evolution

1.1 speciation *[1 mark]*

1.2 The populations can no longer interbreed to produce fertile offspring *[1 mark]*.

2.1 More than 3 billion years ago *[1 mark]*

2.2 New knowledge of fossils *[1 mark]* and geology *[1 mark]*.

2.3 New phenotypes occur because of genetic variants produced by mutations *[1 mark]*.

2.4 Characteristics are passed on in genes from parents to offspring *[1 mark]*.

3 The environment changes too quickly *[1 mark]*. A new predator kills them all *[1 mark]*. A new disease kills them all *[1 mark]*. They can't compete with another new species for food *[1 mark]*. A catastrophic event occurs that kills them all *[1 mark]*.

4 Species show a wide variation in their characteristics because of differences in their alleles/genes *[1 mark]*. In this case, hares with smaller ears have more suitable characteristics for a cold environment because they will lose less heat *[1 mark]*, so are more likely to survive and successfully reproduce *[1 mark]* and pass on the genes controlling smaller ears to the next generation/ their offspring *[1 mark]*. Over time, these genes will have become more common in the species, causing the hares to evolve *[1 mark]*.

Page 104 — More About Evolution

1.1 On the Origin of Species *[1 mark]*

1.2 Because it went against the common religious beliefs at the time about how life on Earth developed / it was the first explanation for the existence of life on Earth without the need for God *[1 mark]*. There also wasn't enough evidence to convince many scientists because not many other studies had been done *[1 mark]*.

1.3 Lamarck believed that changes that an organism acquires during its lifetime will be passed on to its offspring *[1 mark]*.

1.4 E.g. the fossil record, which allows you to see how changes in organisms developed slowly over time *[1 mark]*. The discovery of how bacteria are able to evolve to become resistant to antibiotics *[1 mark]*.

Page 105 — Selective Breeding

1.1 Artificial selection *[1 mark]*

1.2 The breeding of organisms so that the genes for particular useful or attractive characteristics stay in the population *[1 mark]*.

1.3 To produce cows that produce lots of milk/have a high milk yield *[1 mark]*.

Answers

2.1 How to grade your answer:
Level 0: There is no relevant information. *[No marks]*
Level 1: There are some relevant points describing selective breeding but the answer is missing some detail. *[1 to 2 marks]*
Level 2: There is a clear, detailed description of selective breeding that explains how dogs can be selectively bred for good, gentle temperament. *[3 to 4 marks]*
Here are some points your answer may include:
He could have selected two individuals from the population with the best temperaments.
These two individuals would have been bred together.
He would then have selected the individuals from the offspring with the best temperaments and bred them together.
He would have repeated this process over several generations.
This would make the good temperament trait become stronger over time.
Eventually all the puppies would have the good, gentle temperament trait.

2.2 Because selective breeding leads to there being a reduced number of different alleles in the population / a reduced gene pool *[1 mark]*, so there's more chance of the puppies inheriting a genetic defect if it's present in the population *[1 mark]*.

2.3 There is less variation in a selectively bred population *[1 mark]*, so there's less chance of there being any alleles in the population that would give the puppies resistance to the disease *[1 mark]*, so if one individual gets the disease, the others are also likely to succumb to it *[1 mark]*.

Pages 106-107 — Genetic Engineering

Warm-up
False, False, True, True

1.1 The transfer of a gene responsible for a desirable characteristic *[1 mark]* from one organism's genome into another organism's genome *[1 mark]*.

1.2 Enzyme are used to isolate/cut the desired gene from the organism's genome *[1 mark]*.

1.3 The gene is first inserted into a vector *[1 mark]*. The vector is then introduced to the target organism *[1 mark]* and this inserts the gene into the organism's cells so that the organism develops with the desired characteristic *[1 mark]*.

1.4 Any two from: e.g. bacteria have been genetically engineered to produce human insulin that can be used to treat diabetes. / Sheep have been genetically engineered to produce drugs in their milk that can treat human diseases. / Scientists are researching genetic modification treatments (gene therapy) for inherited diseases caused by faulty genes *[2 marks — 1 mark for each correct answer.]*.

2.1 genetically modified *[1 mark]*

2.2 Any two from: e.g. to make them resistant to herbicides. / To make them resistant to disease. / To make them resistant to insects. *[2 marks — 1 mark for each correct answer.]*.

2.3 Mean fruit circumference of Plant 1 =
(16.4 + 16.8 + 15.9 + 16.2 + 15.7 + 16.4 + 16.3 + 16.0 + 15.9 + 16.0) ÷ 10 = **16.2 cm (3 s.f.)** *[1 mark]*
Mean fruit circumference of Plant 2 =
(20.2 + 20.4 + 19.8 + 19.6 + 20.4 + 20.6 + 20.2 + 19.9 + 20.1 + 20.0) ÷ 10 = **20.1 cm (3 s.f.)** *[1 mark]*

2.4 20.1 − 16.2 = 3.9 cm
(3.9 ÷ 16.2) × 100 = **24.1% (3 s.f.)**
[1 mark for correct working, 1 mark for correct answer]
To calculate percentage change, you first need to work out the difference between the two figures. You then need calculate what percentage that difference is of the first figure.

2.5 Any one from: e.g. some people say that growing GM crops will affect the number of wild flowers, and so the population of insects, that live in and around the crops — reducing farmland biodiversity. / Some people are concerned that we might not fully understand the effects of eating GM crops on human health. / People are concerned that transplanted genes might get out into the natural environment. *[1 mark]*

Pages 108-109 — Cloning

1.1 Taking cuttings is an older and simpler method than tissue culture *[1 mark]*.

1.2 Plant cells from the plant being cloned *[1 mark]*.

2.1 E.g. to preserve rare plants that are hard to reproduce naturally *[1 mark]*.

2.2 Disease could wipe out an entire plant population *[1 mark]* because the reduced gene pool resulting from cloning *[1 mark]* reduces the chance of there being an allele in the population that gives the plants resistance to a new disease *[1 mark]*.

3.1 Sperm cells could be taken from the male pig with the desired characteristics and egg cells could be taken from the female pig with the desired characteristics *[1 mark]*. The sperm would be used to artificially fertilise an egg cell *[1 mark]*. The embryo that develops could then be split many times to form clones *[1 mark]* before any of the cells become specialised *[1 mark]*. These cloned embryos could then be implanted into lots of female pigs, where they could develop into identical piglets *[1 mark]*.

3.2 An unfertilised pig egg cell would have its nucleus removed *[1 mark]*. An adult body cell would then be taken from the pig being cloned and its nucleus would be removed *[1 mark]*. The nucleus from the adult body cell would then be inserted into the empty egg cell *[1 mark]*. The egg cell would then be stimulated by an electric shock to make it divide like a normal embryo *[1 mark]*. When the embryo was a ball of cells, it would be implanted into the womb of an adult female pig, where it would develop into a genetically identical copy of the prize-winning pig *[1 mark]*.

Answers

Page 110 — Fossils

Warm-up

False, True, True

1.1 Because decay microbes can't survive in the sap or amber *[1 mark]* as there isn't any oxygen or moisture *[1 mark]*.

1.2 From gradual replacement of parts of an organism by minerals *[1 mark]*. From the preserved casts and impressions of things like burrows/footprints/rootlet traces in a soft material (like clay) *[1 mark]*.

1.3 Many early life-forms were soft bodied and decayed completely, without forming fossils *[1 mark]*. Fossils that did form may have been destroyed by geological activity *[1 mark]*. This means that the fossil record is incomplete *[1 mark]*.

Page 111 — Speciation

1.1 Natural selection *[1 mark]*

1.2 Charles Darwin published 'On the Origin of Species' in 1859 *[1 mark]*.

1.3 warning colouration *[1 mark]*

2 Environmental conditions for each population will be slightly different and so natural selection will act differently on each population *[1 mark]*. The genetic variation between individuals in each population will mean that some individuals are better adapted than others to their new environment *[1 mark]*. These individuals have a better chance of survival, so are more likely to breed successfully *[1 mark]*, passing on the alleles that control the beneficial characteristics *[1 mark]*. Eventually, individuals from the different populations will have changed so much that they won't be able to breed with each other to produce fertile offspring, so will have become separate species *[1 mark]*.

Pages 112-113 — Antibiotic-Resistant Bacteria

1.1 E.g when they are prescribed for viral infections *[1 mark]* or non-serious conditions *[1 mark]*.

1.2 Because this ensures that all bacteria are destroyed *[1 mark]*, so there are none left to mutate *[1 mark]* and develop into antibiotic-resistant strains *[1 mark]*.

2.1 Because the rate of development of new antibiotics is slow *[1 mark]* and it is a costly process *[1 mark]*.

2.2 Bacteria develop random mutations in their DNA *[1 mark]*, some of which lead to the bacteria becoming less affected by antibiotics *[1 mark]*. These bacteria are better able to survive and reproduce in hosts undergoing antibiotic treatment *[1 mark]*, meaning that the gene becomes more common in the population, forming antibiotic-resistant strains *[1 mark]*. As there is no effective treatment for these strains, they can spread very easily between individuals *[1 mark]*.

3.1 How to grade your answer:

Level 0: There is no relevant information. *[No marks]*

Level 1: There is a brief description of a method that could be used to carry out the investigation. Very little detail is included and some steps may be in the wrong order. *[1 to 2 marks]*

Level 2: There is a good description of a method that could be used to carry out the investigation. Some detail is missing, but all of the steps are in a sensible order. *[3 to 4 marks]*

Level 3: There is a clear and detailed description of a method that could be used to carry out the investigation. All of the steps are in a sensible order. *[5 to 6 marks]*

Here are some points your answer may include:

Use a sterile pipette to measure out equal volumes of sterile nutrient broth solution into four sterile glass bottles.

Use another sterile pipette to add equal volumes of ampicillin solution to two of the glass bottles.

Use another sterile pipette to transfer some of strain A to one bottle with ampicillin in it and one bottle without ampicillin.

Use another sterile pipette to transfer some of strain B to one bottle with ampicillin and one bottle without ampicillin.

Set up a control experiment without bacteria / just broth solution and the antibiotic.

Put lids on all of the bottles. Store them all at the same temperature for a few days.

Observe each bottle to see if the nutrient broth solution has gone cloudy.

3.2 E.g. if strain B is resistant to ampicillin, it may cause bacterial infections that are difficult to treat if it is released into the general population, so it must be disposed of properly. / The bacteria used may pose a health risk to humans if not disposed of properly. / If the antibiotic used is not disposed of properly it may be released into the environment, where other bacteria may develop resistance to it *[1 mark]*.

Page 114 — Classification

1.1 E.g. current classification data *[1 mark]* and information from the fossil record *[1 mark]*.

1.2 B *[1 mark]*

1.3 G and H *[1 mark]*

2.1 kingdom, phylum, class, order, family, genus, species *[1 mark]*

2.2 (Carl) Woese *[1 mark]*

2.3 plants *[1 mark]*, animals *[1 mark]*, protists *[1 mark]*

Answers

Topic 7 — Ecology

Page 115 — Competition

1.1 the soil *[1 mark]*
1.2 light *[1 mark]* and space *[1 mark]*
1.3 Any three from: space/territory / food / water / mates *[3 marks]*.
2.1 interdependence *[1 mark]*
2.2 E.g. the number of blue tits might decrease *[1 mark]* because there would be no caterpillars for them to eat *[1 mark]*. The numbers of plants might increase *[1 mark]* because there would be no caterpillars to eat them *[1 mark]*.
2.3 A stable community is one where all the species and environmental factors are in balance *[1 mark]* so that the population sizes remain fairly constant *[1 mark]*.

Pages 116-117 — Abiotic and Biotic Factors

1.1 Light intensity, temperature and carbon dioxide level are all examples of abiotic factors. *[1 mark]*
The other answers are incorrect because they mix up examples of biotic and abiotic factors. Remember, abiotic factors are non-living factors and biotic factors are living factors.
1.2 E.g. oxygen level *[1 mark]*.
1.3 Any two from: e.g. moisture level / soil pH / soil mineral content / carbon dioxide level *[2 marks]*.
2 E.g. because the grey and red squirrels were in competition *[1 mark]* for the same resources such as food and shelter *[1 mark]*. The grey squirrels out-competed the red squirrels *[1 mark]*.
3 The birds would not be feeding on the insects *[1 mark]*, so insects would breed and increase in numbers *[1 mark]*. More insects would eat more grass so the grass plant numbers might decrease *[1 mark]*.
4.1 Both populations increase then decrease sharply, then increase again over the ten years *[1 mark]*. The heron population starts to decrease and increase slightly later than the perch population *[1 mark]*.
4.2 The average pH of the lake fell between years 4 and 5 *[1 mark]*. Possibly not all of the perch could survive in the more acidic water *[1 mark]*. The data cannot confirm the reason because there might have been another abiotic or biotic factor that affected the perch population *[1 mark]*.
You still get the second mark here if you came up with any other sensible reason why the fall in the pH of the water might have caused the perch population to decrease.
4.3 E.g. there might be other fish/prey in the lake, which aren't affected by the disease, that the herons can eat *[1 mark]*. The other fish/prey might have more food if the perch population falls, so their populations will increase *[1 mark]*. So the herons might still have as much food as before *[1 mark]*.

Pages 118-119 — Adaptations

1.1 extremophiles *[1 mark]*
1.2 bacteria *[1 mark]*
1.3 high pressure *[1 mark]*
2.1 Long eyelashes stop sand getting into the eyes *[1 mark]*. Large feet stop the camel sinking into the sand / make it easier for the camel to walk in sand *[1 mark]*.
2.2 It reduces water loss *[1 mark]*.
2.3 A swollen stem stores water *[1 mark]*.
2.4 Shallow, wide-spreading roots allow water to be absorbed over a larger area *[1 mark]* while long, deep roots allow the plant to absorb water from deep below the surface *[1 mark]*.
3.1 E.g. they would seek shade *[1 mark]*.
3.2 dark coloured skin *[1 mark]*
3.3 functional adaptation *[1 mark]*

Page 120 — Food Chains

Warm-up
        producer — seaweed, secondary consumer — shark
1.1 primary consumer *[1 mark]*
1.2 They produce glucose *[1 mark]* by carrying out photosynthesis *[1 mark]*. They then use this glucose to make biological molecules that make up the plant's biomass *[1 mark]*.
2.1 The number of lynx increases *[1 mark]* because the number of snowshoe hares is increasing and so they have lots of food *[1 mark]*.
2.2 An increase in the number of lynx, which mean more hares are eaten *[1 mark]*.

Page 121 — Using Quadrats

1.1 It avoids the data being biased *[1 mark]*.
1.2 13 buttercups *[1 mark]*
1.3 15.5 buttercups *[1 mark]*
1.4 $(15 + 13 + 16 + 23 + 26 + 23 + 13 + 12 + 16 + 13)$ $\div 10 = 170 \div 10 = $ **17 buttercups per 0.5 m²** *[1 mark]*
1.5 Mean number of buttercups per m² = $17 \times 2 = 34$
Estimated population size = mean number of buttercups per m² × total area of the field in m²
Estimated population size = 34×1750
= **59 500 buttercups** *[3 marks for correct answer, otherwise 1 mark for '34 buttercups per m²' and 1 mark for '34 × 1750'.]*

Pages 122-123 — Using Transects

1.1 Zones B and C. *[1 mark]*
1.2 long grass *[1 mark]*
1.3 Zone A is closest to the pond where the soil has more moisture *[1 mark]*. Zone A also has a higher light intensity *[1 mark]*.
1.4 Zone B *[1 mark]* because only short grass grows in zone B *[1 mark]*.
1.5 The light levels may be too low. / The moisture level may be too low. *[1 mark]*

Answers

1.6 Record the number of times each of the four species touch the transect line. / Count the number of species/ measure the percentage cover of each species using a quadrat placed along the transect. *[1 mark]*

2.1 E.g. the ground might be slippery / there might be large waves from the sea / the tide might come in *[1 mark]*.
Any sensible suggestion of a hazard you might find at a beach would get you the mark for this question.

2.2 Advantage: e.g. you can cover a larger distance in the same amount of time / it takes less time to collect data from along the transect *[1 mark]*.
Disadvantage: e.g. the results might not be as accurate / some species might get missed *[1 mark]*.

2.3 The percentage cover of bladderwrack increases between 2 m and 18 m from the low tide point / the further the distance from the low tide point, the higher the percentage cover of bladderwrack, up to 18 m *[1 mark]*. The percentage cover then falls between 18 m and 20 m *[1 mark]*.

2.4 E.g. they could measure the salt concentration of the water around the bladderwrack at each interval *[1 mark]*.

Page 124 — Environmental Change & The Water Cycle

Warm-up

evaporate, water vapour, cools, precipitation

1.1 one *[1 mark]*

1.2 The further away from the road the greater the number of lichen species *[1 mark]*, because the concentration of sulfur dioxide from cars gets lower further from the road *[1 mark]*.

1.3 25 m *[1 mark]*

Page 125 — The Carbon Cycle

1.1 photosynthesis *[1 mark]*

1.2 (green) plants *[1 mark]*

1.3 burning *[1 mark]*

1.4 Any one from: e.g. leather / wool. *[1 mark]*

1.5 Carbon dioxide is returned back to the atmosphere *[1 mark]* when the microorganisms involved in decay respire *[1 mark]*.

Page 126 — Decay

Warm-up

Grass cuttings and food peelings.

1.1 methane *[1 mark]*

1.2 Biogas is produced by anaerobic decay. *[1 mark]*

1.3 To keep the temperature in the generator steady / to protect the generator from extremes of temperature *[1 mark]*.

1.4 As a fertiliser / to add nutrients to the soil *[1 mark]*.

1.5 It should be warm / not too hot or too cold *[1 mark]*. There should be water/moisture available *[1 mark]*. There should be lots of oxygen available *[1 mark]*.

Page 127 — Investigating Decay

1.1 From pink to colourless.
Phenolphthalein itself changes from pink to colourless, but because the rest of the contents of the tube are white, the colour of the mixture in the tube goes from pink to white.

1.2 $$\text{mean} = \frac{(217 + 224 + 219)}{3}$$
$$= \textbf{220 seconds } \textit{[1 mark]}$$

1.3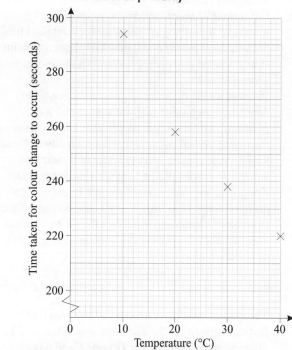

[2 marks for all four points plotted correctly, otherwise 1 mark for 2 points plotted correctly.]

1.4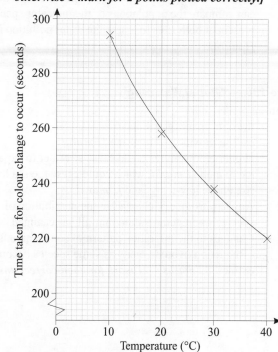

[1 mark for a smooth curve of best fit that passes through or as near to as many points as possible.]

1.5 228 seconds *[1 mark]*
Your curve of best fit may differ slightly so accept any answer between 226 and 230 seconds as long as the curve of best fit has been read from correctly.

Answers

Pages 128-129 — Biodiversity and Waste Management

1.1 The variety of different species of organisms on Earth, or within an ecosystem. *[1 mark]*

1.2 E.g. deforestation / waste production *[1 mark]*.

2.1 The human population is growing *[1 mark]* and the standard of living is increasing *[1 mark]*.

2.2 Any two from: e.g. sewage / fertilisers / pesticides / herbicides *[2 marks]*.

2.3 E.g. smoke *[1 mark]* and acidic gases *[1 mark]*.

3.1 It reduces the variety of plants on the land (by killing the weeds) *[1 mark]* and it may kill plants and animals if it is washed into nearby water / it pollutes nearby water *[1 mark]*.

3.2 Because all the different species in the ecosystem depend on each other (e.g. for shelter and food) *[1 mark]*. Different species can also help to maintain the right physical environment for each other *[1 mark]*.

4.1 River 2 has a higher level of water pollution than River 1 *[1 mark]*. River 2 contains more rat-tailed maggots than River 1, and these are found in highly polluted water *[1 mark]*. River 2 also contains fewer freshwater shrimp and water lice than River 1, and these are found in water with a medium or low level of pollution *[1 mark]*.

You'd also get the marks here for explaining this the other way round — for describing how you can tell that River 1 has a lower level of pollution than River 2.

4.2 The student would need to survey one area that is just downstream of the discharge site, which will be affected by the waste water *[1 mark]*, and one area that is just upstream of the discharge site, where no waste water is present *[1 mark]*. Then the student can compare the populations of the indicator species present at both sites to assess the water pollution levels *[1 mark]*.

Page 130 — Global Warming

Warm-up

the Sun, space, gases, increases

1.1 carbon dioxide and methane *[1 mark]*

1.2 Higher temperatures could cause seawater to expand / ice to melt *[1 mark]*, which could cause the sea level to rise above low-lying land *[1 mark]*.

1.3 Any two from: e.g. changes in the distribution of species where temperature/rainfall has changed. / Changes to the migration pattern of some animals. / Reduction in biodiversity as some species become extinct. *[2 marks — 1 mark for each correct answer.]*

Page 131 — Deforestation and Land Use

1 Any two from: e.g. building / farming / quarrying / dumping waste *[2 marks — 1 mark for each correct answer]*.

2.1 E.g. to use the land as farmland. / To use the peat as compost. *[1 mark]*

2.2 Carbon dioxide is released *[1 mark]*, which contributes to global warming *[1 mark]*.

2.3 It reduces biodiversity *[1 mark]* because it destroys habitats / reduces the area of habitats *[1 mark]*.

3.1 To clear land to grow the crops needed to produce biofuels *[1 mark]*.

3.2 E.g. to provide land for cattle (to raise for food) *[1 mark]*. To provide land to grow crops, e.g. rice (to provide more food) *[1 mark]*.

4 Any two from: e.g. it increases the amount of carbon dioxide in the atmosphere *[1 mark]* because carbon dioxide is released by burning wood and the decomposing of wood by microorganisms *[1 mark]*. / It reduces the rate at which carbon dioxide is removed from the atmosphere *[1 mark]* because there are fewer trees taking it up for photosynthesis *[1 mark]*. / It leads to a reduction in biodiversity in the area *[1 mark]* because trees/habitats are destroyed *[1 mark]*.

Page 132 — Maintaining Ecosystems and Biodiversity

1.1 Burning fewer fossil fuels. *[1 mark]*

1.2 E.g. this could reduce the amount of land taken over for landfill *[1 mark]*, leaving ecosystems in place *[1 mark]*.

2.1 It decreases biodiversity *[1 mark]*, because the habitat wouldn't be able to support a wide range of organisms *[1 mark]*.

2.2 The strips of grassland and hedgerows increase the biodiversity by providing more habitats / food sources *[1 mark]*.

3 E.g. it costs money to protect biodiversity (and make sure that the programmes are being followed) and some people may feel that the money should be spent on other things *[1 mark]*. Protecting biodiversity may have a negative impact on local people's livelihood (e.g. if they're employed in tree-felling), which could affect the local economy *[1 mark]*. Some people (e.g. farmers) may want to kill organisms that are regarded as pests to protect crops and livestock *[1 mark]*. Some people may want to use land for new housing or agricultural land *[1 mark]*.

Answers

Page 133 — Trophic Levels

Warm-up

Producer	Herbivore	Carnivore
plankton algae	barnacle limpet winkle	dog whelk crab gull

1.1 herbivores *[1 mark]*
1.2 level 4 *[1 mark]*
1.3 A carnivore that has no predators *[1 mark]*.
2 Decomposers break down/recycle any dead plant or animal material in the environment *[1 mark]*. They do this by secreting enzymes *[1 mark]* which break down the dead material into small soluble molecules *[1 mark]*. They take up these molecules by diffusion *[1 mark]*.

Pages 134-135 — Pyramids of Biomass

1.1

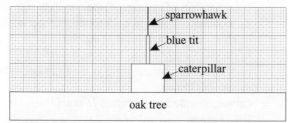

[1 mark for pyramid of biomass constructed with trophic level 1 at the bottom of the pyramid. 2 marks for all four trophic levels plotted correctly to scale, otherwise 1 mark for three trophic levels plotted correctly to scale. 1 mark for correctly labelled bars (and axis if one is used).]

1.2 The biomass decreases as the trophic level increases *[1 mark]*, so there's not enough energy/biomass to support more trophic levels *[1 mark]*.
2.1 The biomass of the whole plant isn't being measured — e.g. dig up the whole plant, including the roots and leaves *[1 mark]*.
The plant may not be fully dried — e.g. weigh the plant at intervals while it is being dried and keep drying it until the mass is constant for three measurements *[1 mark]*.
The sampling isn't representative of the whole field — e.g. place the quadrat at randomly selected points on the field *[1 mark]*.
2.2 A larger sample size is likely to be more representative of the whole dandelion population *[1 mark]*. It will also make it easier to spot any anomalies/errors in her measurements *[1 mark]*.
2.3 E.g. the student has to remove the plants from the field to measure the biomass. Removing too many could negatively affect the ecosystem *[1 mark]*.
2.4 E.g. cuts from equipment used to dig up/cut dandelions / tripping hazards on the ground in the field / burns from the oven *[1 mark]*.

Page 136 — Biomass Transfer

1.1 It will be egested as faeces *[1 mark]*.
1.2 E.g. urea *[1 mark]*, water *[1 mark]*.
2.1 Glucose *[1 mark]* is used in respiration to provide energy, rather than to make biomass *[1 mark]*. Also, respiration produces carbon dioxide and water as waste products *[1 mark]* which are lost from the body and therefore not passed on as biomass *[1 mark]*.
2.2 $(0.60 \div 6.40) \times 100 = 0.09375 \times 100 = 9.375$
= **9.38% (3 s.f.)** *[2 marks for correct answer, otherwise 1 mark for correct working.]*
2.3 $(11.6 + 9.38 + 10.0) \div 3$ *[1 mark]*
= **10.3 (3 s.f.)** *[1 mark]*

If you get the wrong answer for the first part of a calculation question and then have to use that value in a following question part (like you do above) it's unlikely that you'll lose marks for getting the wrong answer for the second part due to using the wrong value (as long as all your working is correct). So it's worth giving all parts of the question a go, even if you're not sure whether your answer to the first part is correct... and make sure you always write down your working.

Pages 137-138 — Food Security and Farming

1.1 Decreasing birth rate. *[1 mark]*
1.2 E.g. reduction of rainfall *[1 mark]*.
2.1 To prevent species from disappearing *[1 mark]*.
2.2 E.g. there are limits on how small the mesh sizes of nets can be *[1 mark]* and fishing quotas have been introduced *[1 mark]*.
3.1 It reduces the transfer of energy from the fish to the environment *[1 mark]*, meaning that more energy is available for growth *[1 mark]*.
3.2 Carnivorous fish are a higher trophic level than plant-eating fish *[1 mark]*, so more biomass/energy will have been lost from the food chain by that level (because there are more trophic levels) *[1 mark]*.
3.3 E.g. disease is spread more easily between closely-packed animals *[1 mark]*.
4.1 Chicken *[1 mark]* because it requires the least amount of feed to produce 1 kg of meat *[1 mark]*.
4.2 chicken : cattle = 2.1 : 10.5.
2.1 ÷ 2.1 = 1.   10.5 ÷ 2.1 = 5
So the ratio in its simplest form is **1 : 5** *[1 mark]*.
4.3 It could decrease/weaken global food security *[1 mark]* because more crops are needed to produce more meat to meet the increasing demand *[1 mark]*, so there are fewer crops / less land for crops available to produce food for the global population *[1 mark]*.

Page 139 — Biotechnology

1.1 E.g. producing human insulin *[1 mark]*.
1.2 E.g. they could provide more food *[1 mark]* and they could provide food with an improved nutritional value (such as Golden Rice) *[1 mark]*.
2.1 *Fusarium* *[1 mark]*
2.2 aerobic *[1 mark]*
2.3 glucose *[1 mark]*
2.4 purification of the product *[1 mark]*

Answers

Mixed Questions

Pages 140-146 — Mixed Questions

1.1 E.g. producing bile / converting lactic acid to glucose / storing glucose as glycogen / breaking down amino acids *[1 mark]*.

1.2 Enzymes speed up chemical reactions in living organisms. *[1 mark]*.

1.3 pH 9 *[1 mark]*

1.4 The enzyme will not work *[1 mark]* because the acid will change the shape of its active site/denature the enzyme *[1 mark]* and the substrate will no longer fit *[1 mark]*.

1.5 Alcohol is a risk factor for lung cancer. *[1 mark]*

2.1 To stop the loss of water by evaporation *[1 mark]*.

2.2
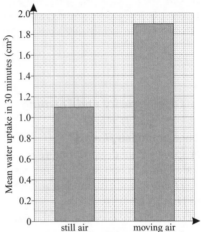

[1 mark for correctly drawn bars, one mark for correctly labelled axes.]

2.3 The greater the air flow around the plant, the greater the transpiration rate *[1 mark]*.

2.4 E.g. increasing air flow carries more water vapour away from the plant / reduces the concentration of water vapour outside the leaves *[1 mark]*. This increases the rate of diffusion of water from the leaf cells from an area of higher water concentration to an area of lower water concentration *[1 mark]*.

2.5 1.2 − 0.8 = **0.4 cm³** *[1 mark]*
The range is the difference between the highest and lowest values.

2.6 30 minutes ÷ 60 = 0.5 hours
1.9 ÷ 0.5 = **3.8 cm³/hour** *[2 marks for correct answer, otherwise 1 mark for correct working.]*

3.1 mitochondria *[1 mark]*

3.2 glucose + oxygen → carbon dioxide + water
[1 mark for both reactants correct, 1 mark for both products correct.]

3.3 Glucose is combined with nitrate ions *[1 mark]* to make amino acids *[1 mark]*, which are then joined together to make proteins *[1 mark]*.

4.1 The hormone is secreted directly into the blood *[1 mark]*. It is then carried in the blood to the target organ *[1 mark]*.

4.2 C *[1 mark]*

4.3 B *[1 mark]*

4.4 It stimulates ovulation / the release of an egg from an ovary *[1 mark]*.

4.5 ovaries *[1 mark]*

4.6 A constantly high level of oestrogen inhibits the production of FSH *[1 mark]*, so there are no mature eggs for fertilisation to take place *[1 mark]*.

5.1 oxygen *[1 mark]*

5.2 light intensity *[1 mark]*

5.3 Tube 1 *[1 mark]*

5.4 Tube 1 shows that in the dark, the algae are producing more carbon dioxide than they take in *[1 mark]*. The concentration of carbon dioxide is high because the cells are respiring, but not photosynthesising (as there's no light for photosynthesis to take place) *[1 mark]*. Tube 2 shows that in the light, the algae are taking up more carbon dioxide than they produce *[1 mark]*. The concentration of carbon dioxide has reduced because the cells are photosynthesising faster than they are respiring *[1 mark]*.

5.5 Any two from: e.g. the temperature of the boiling tubes / the volume of hydrogencarbonate indicator / the concentration of hydrogencarbonate indicator / the number of beads in each tube / the concentration of algal cells in each bead *[2 marks]*.

5.6 Light intensity *[1 mark]* because the rate of photosynthesis is increasing as the light intensity increases *[1 mark]*.

5.7 carbon dioxide concentration *[1 mark]*

6.1 RR *[1 mark]*

6.2 round seed shape *[1 mark]*

6.3

	Ⓡ	Ⓡ
ⓡ	Rr	Rr
ⓡ	Rr	Rr

[1 mark]
Genotypes: **RR** *[1 mark]* and **rr** *[1 mark]*.

7.1 E.g. using mosquito nets (to prevent biting) *[1 mark]*.

7.2 mitosis *[1 mark]*

7.3 There are fewer red blood cells to carry oxygen to all the cells in the body *[1 mark]*. This means that the cells aren't receiving enough oxygen for respiration/ transferring energy from glucose *[1 mark]*.

7.4 E.g. a flushing agent is used to help the blood sample flow from one end of the stick to the other through the paper strip *[1 mark]*.

7.5 Antibodies complementary to the malaria antigen are stuck to the strip at point B *[1 mark]*. Malaria antigens bound to the dye-labelled antibodies have flowed along the strip from point A to point B *[1 mark]* where they have bound to antibodies that are stuck to the strip *[1 mark]*. Because the antibodies containing dye have bound at point B they are visible there as a coloured line *[1 mark]*.